Animals Are Not Ours
(No, *Really*, They're Not)

Animals Are Not Ours

(No, *Really*, They're Not)

AN EVANGELICAL ANIMAL LIBERATION THEOLOGY

Sarah Withrow King

CASCADE *Books* · Eugene, Oregon

ANIMALS ARE NOT OURS (NO, REALLY, THEY'RE NOT)
An Evangelical Animal Liberation Theology

Cascade Books
An Imprint of Wipf and Stock Publishers
199 W. 8th Ave., Suite 3
Eugene, OR 97401

www.wipfandstock.com

ISBN 13: 978-1-4982-0180-3

Cataloguing-in-Publication Data

King, Sarah Withrow

Animals are not ours (no, really, they're not) : an evangelical animal liberation theology / Sarah Withrow King.

x + 184 p. ; 23 cm. Includes bibliographical references and index.

ISBN 13: 978-1-4982-0180-3

1. Animal welfare—Religious aspects—Christianity. 2. Animals—Religious aspects—Christianity. I. Title.

BT746 .K54 2016

Manufactured in the U.S.A.   12/31/2015

PETA—Feeding the World infographic
ESA—*Peace Begins on Our Plates* (reprint from PRISM Magazine)

For Isaiah—may the world you inherit be one of justice, kindness, humility, and love

Contents

Acknowledgments

First, thanksgiving for a few lovely people:

- Nicole Morgan read initial drafts of some chapters and provided very helpful feedback, then ensured that all my i's were dotted and t's were crossed, for which I am extremely grateful

- Tracy Reiman, who saw and nurtured me before I was able to

- Ron Sider, Al Tizon, Kristyn Komarnicki, Rhian Tomassetti, and Josh Cradic: colleagues at Evangelicals for Social Action who were constant cheerleaders, and who made me laugh as I balanced work with writing with family with life

- The staff, professors, and students of Palmer Theological Seminary, who challenged and encouraged me as I wrestled through the theological issues in the following pages

- The Circle of Hope community in Philadelphia, for really being the church

And a few longer, slightly mushier thanksgivings:

Sure, I have struggled with depression for much of my life, but my parents have provided endless emotional and physical support—and though no one is perfect, I grew up thinking that I could do anything I put my mind to, believing that I had a good brain in my head, and knowing way deep down inside that God and my parents loved me very much.

My dad, Rolland, read and gave extensive feedback on early drafts of Part One. I always appreciate it when someone will give really good critical input, and he did that.

My mom, Jeanne, has reminded me over and over again to take a deep breath and give my anxiety and fear to God. I have always admired her quiet faithfulness.

Paul Alexander—professor, boss, mentor, and friend—thank you. Thank you. Thank you. You helped me trust my voice, introduced me to theologies and ways of knowing God that I hadn't thought possible, and have made me laugh and cry and question and love. You are as awesome as you think I am.

And Giehl. There are no words to express the depth of my gratitude for your many, many sacrifices over the last few years. Thank you for taking care of our home, our child, and me. Thank you for supporting my call to seminary, and for making it possible for me to finish that journey. I love you and our wacky little life.

Introduction

An Ode to Meat

I LOVE MEAT. L-O-V-E it. I used to eat a couple of sausage-and-egg McMuffins for breakfast and a Dagwood-style deli sandwich for lunch every day (is there really anything much better to eat than a perfect sandwich?). For dinner, I loved all God's creatures, right next to my mashed potatoes (or French fries) and some limp broccoli smothered in cheese sauce: salmon, trout, halibut, crab, clam, lobster, shrimp, cow, bison, deer, rabbit, chicken, turkey, pig, and lamb. My favorite snack was salami and cheese on crackers, most abundant around the holidays. When we were young, we often went to a buffet restaurant with my grandma and grandpa for dinner on Fridays. It was a smorgasbord of meat, all different ways. My favorite salad was a Cobb—two kinds of meat, plus eggs and cheese. Church cookouts and pot-lucks and Wednesday night dinners were always satisfying.

When I was around ten years old, someone handed me a leaflet outside of the Albertsons where we did our grocery shopping. It described where veal came from, and I felt pretty bad for the baby cows, tied up for weeks in little cages, so I never ate veal again . . . well, until I really wanted a calzone that had a little veal mashed in with the sausage and beef. "No big deal," I thought. Under the influence of a nerdy-cute camp counselor, I gave up meat for Lent one year—but forgot my vow when I went to Subway for lunch with my girlfriends. I didn't think of my turkey sub as having meat on it. For the first six months I was vegan, all I wanted, every day, was a bacon cheeseburger.

I really like meat.

Confusion to Contempt to Compassion

I didn't just really like meat; I thought it was bizarre that anyone would choose not to eat it. At my seventh-grade birthday party, all we could think of to feed my one vegetarian friend was salad. What else do vegetarians eat, right? I have been paid back for that early ignorance in spades—every time the vegetarian option is a plate of steamed vegetables, or I am asked to bring my own food to a function, or someone offers fish instead of "meat."

Eventually, I moved from confusion to contempt, making fun of my friend Beau when he ordered a meatless burrito from a fast-food taco place, and mercilessly mocking my vegan friend Matt when he refused to eat a bean burrito that had mistakenly been made with cheese. Now, I smile graciously when someone learns I'm vegan and takes extra pains to describe their carnivorous ways, or when, for the 195th time, a jolly grandfather type at church invites my husband and me over for steaks (sigh).

So how did this meat-loving evangelical girl from Idaho end up working at the world's largest and most notorious animal rights organization, People for the Ethical Treatment of Animals (PETA)? I've been an activist since I was old enough to walk. At four, my parents took me to a pro-life rally at the Idaho capitol building, and our picture made the front page of the Boise newspaper. In middle school, I was president of a drug education club with the unfortunate acronym OSSOM (Oregon Student Safety on the Move). In high school, I presided over the local Teens for Life group, tabled for Oregon Right to Life at local events, performed pro-life songs and plays at rallies, and attended statewide pro-life conferences. I had a strong sense of justice, of the clear line between right and wrong. Though some of that righteous indignation was the byproduct of teenage know-it-all-itis, it was also fueled in part by my evangelical beliefs. I was raised in the church, had read the Bible front to back multiple times, spent all my spare time in youth group, was baptized, went on mission trips, prayed a decent amount, and thought I understood the Bible clearly. I also knew that God had called me to stand up for justice and life in the face of a culture that systematically finds ways to prevent lives from flourishing.

During college, when my brother was vegan, I went to a vegan restaurant with him and picked up a pamphlet that was left out on our table. I started to read about factory farming and the way that billions of animals that end up on North-American plates are raised and slaughtered. My images of happy animals on Old MacDonald's farm were shattered and replaced with dark new ones: miserable lives all ending in the same nightmarish way, hung upside down on a fast-moving slaughter line, throat slit, waiting to die. It took about a year, but eventually I stopped being able to look at the chicken on my plate as food and started to realize that when I ate meat, my meal had stopped a beating heart. I lived on death.

Animals Are Not Ours

By the time I graduated from college, I had a fair bit of painful life experience behind me: a series of moves, multiple bouts of serious depression, a marriage broken beyond repair, and mounds of personal and student debt. The years since high school had also radically shifted my faith. My relationship with Jesus was personal now—raw and real. I'd been through the valleys of the shadow of death and Jesus had walked beside me, picked me up and carried me through to another side. The overflow of mercy and grace helped me show others mercy, as well. I was (am) still a judgmental jerk, but less so, and with a great deal more humility. Some folks say that not eating animals makes them kinder, less angry, more compassionate. Jesus did that for me . . . well, I'm a slow learner, so Jesus is still doing that for me, day by day.

Both of my parents had jobs in the insurance industry, and I, being young and judgmental, wanted to do something different, to work for a cause. Thankfully, I don't mind being broke all the time. I started my job search by making a long list of organizations that I thought I would feel good working for, then ranking them. My friend Matt (the vegan one that I made fun of in high school—he was nicer to me than I had been to him and kept being friends with me) told me about this organization called PETA, and I went to their website to see what they were all about. My life changed that day.

I was sitting in my mom's office in the house I had grown up in, in Eugene, Oregon. It was a warm August morning and her desk was cluttered with my organizational research and résumé material, household bills, correspondence, and photos. My heart started racing when I read the PETA motto: "Animals are not ours to eat, wear, experiment on, or use for entertainment." My face felt flush as I read it over and over again, and I began to feel a deep joy, a connection with the words, which articulated what my soul had understood for so long already. They're not ours. It would take me nearly eleven years to articulate in theological terms the Spirit-truth that overpowered me that morning.

Orientation

PETA moved to the top of my list of organizations I wanted to work for. On October 4, 2002, I wrote, "On the day after my birthday, I'll be flying to Norfolk to interview for a policy research position with PETA. I'm *very* excited and, well, rendered a little speechless that I landed an interview at my dream job so quickly and from so far away. Anyway, it's a big blessing. This is something that I'm *very* passionate about, but have always felt so helpless . . ."

By the last day of the three-day interview, I was more determined than ever to work for PETA. I had met with PETA President Ingrid Newkirk on my first day in the office and shown her my portfolio, dutifully prepared and printed on (I can't believe I'm admitting this) Noah's ark–themed paper. To demonstrate my commitment to the mission of the organization, my portfolio claimed, "While many injustices of the world inspire a passionate response from me, none is stronger than the pure, visceral dismay registered at the thought of various human abuses of animals." I showed her the aforementioned front-page picture of bundled and bespeckled four-year-old me on my dad's shoulders at a right-to-life rally in Boise (activist cred!). Four days after I returned home to Eugene, I wrote in my journal, "!!!!! I GOT IT!!!!"

Two weeks later, I checked two big boxes and carried my cat, Max, through security at Portland International Airport. That Thursday, I started at PETA. I had never felt more secure, more confident, and more certain that I was living into God's call for my life. I felt God's presence and careful watch every day and night. With no car, no apartment, no furniture, and few belongings, I began a brand new life in Norfolk, Virginia, completely dependent on God to provide. And God provided in abundance. A tiny attic apartment, hand-me-down furniture, frequent rides to thrift stores and grocery stores and the vet, friends who became my nuclear family, and a church family who eventually introduced me to my husband and encouraged my journey to Palmer Theological Seminary.

My date book from that time is full until December 16 and 17 of 2002. On those days, starting at noon each day, is simply written "ORIENTA-TION." During orientation, each of the major departments came to give a brief presentation on their work to new employees, not so different from the orientations I had received at various hotels where I had worked. But, since a picture is worth a thousand words, the presentations at PETA were frequently accompanied by videos.

I should pause here—before this, even when I ate animals, I did not watch animal movies. Or read books about animals. I knew the animal always got the short end of the stick. At a youth-group lock-in, when the first few frames of *Where the Red Fern Grows* popped up on the movie screen and I saw two sweet-looking dogs, I forced myself to sleep in the middle of a packed, fully lit room to avoid watching the film (I've still never seen it but can guess that it doesn't end well for the dogs). I excused myself from a friend's living room when her family sat down to watch *Old Yeller* together and hung out on her front porch for the duration of the movie.

What I saw during those two orientation days has stayed with me for more than a decade.

Baby elephants in Thailand, dragged screaming from their mothers, tied up and beaten with nail-studded sticks for days until their spirits and bodies are so broken that they can be trained to carry tourists. Elephants, tigers, and lions used by circuses here in the U.S., beaten with bullhooks, punched, and burned to force them to do stupid tricks in front of throngs of screaming children, who would scream in horror if they knew the pain endured by the animals they love.

Cats in China, boiled alive and skinned, tossed back into pots of water, air bubbles from their noses indicating that they are still alive, slowly dying. Mice, heads cut off with a pair of scissors by a lab assistant. Mother rats shoved into tubes and forced to breathe cigarette smoke to prove again what we already know.

Beagles in a pharmaceutical lab, slowly being poisoned to death—struggling to stand, foaming at the mouth, given only the insufficient grace of a loving touch by the hand of an undercover investigator. Mother dogs in stacked wire cages in puppy mills—matted and filthy, pus and blood oozing from wounds. This is what we do to dogs, the human's closest and most loyal companion.

A beaver struggling for ten minutes in an underwater trap before finally drowning. Foxes, wolves, dogs, and squirrels mangled by leg-hold traps, finally bludgeoned or stomped to death when the trapper returns to check the line. Minks in cages, spinning wildly, out of their minds with boredom, then anally or vaginally electrocuted so their skins can be made into coats for the very wealthy or fur trim for wealthy wannabes.

And thirteen long minutes of standard agricultural practices like castration, dehorning, tail docking, tooth pulling, branding, and debeaking (all without anesthetic); overcrowding; gestation crates and veal crates;

packed and terrifying transport trucks; and bloody, dark slaughterhouses where, no matter how loud the animals' screams become, the line never slows . . .[1]

After those two days, there are no more notes, no more to-dos, and no more appointments. Those two afternoons turned my adventure into a focused, desperate attempt to stem cruelty and abuse, the depth, breadth, and depravity of which I had never fathomed.

A few years later, I was representing PETA at a Christian music festival in central Washington. My colleague and I were showing the same thirteen-minute video that I had watched during orientation and talking to attendees about why animal issues mattered to us and melded with our faith. I explained to one man (a chaperone) that twenty-seven billion animals were killed for food in the U.S. alone each year. His response to me was "thank God for that." I realized that although my personal faith was stronger than ever, I had no theological framework from which to articulate what I knew to be true—that animals aren't ours.

I hope this book can be a resource for those who care about animals and hate what humans do to them, yet aren't sure how to stop contributing to cruelty or how to talk about the issues from a Jesus point of view. And I offer thanks to the theologians who have come before me, especially Andrew Linzey, who has been a pioneer in this field for decades, and David Clough, who recently wrote the first systematic animal theology. While this book represents my best thinking on the subject today, I know I have much to learn still and am grateful for these and other teachers.

My Cre(e)d

I don't eat meat, a choice that is consistent with my understanding of the nature of Jesus's life and death as it relates to the coming of the kingdom of God, in which all creation will be reconciled to the Creator. Jesus Christ, God incarnate, suffered through and triumphed over death. Jesus's life and ministry inform my own. His living, dying, and rising brought the kingdom of God to earth, though we are not yet fully reconciled to one another or to the Creator. We created beings therefore have the extraordinary opportunity and immense responsibility to be agents of kingdom promises—we look forward to a time when "the people who walk in darkness [will see] a great light" (Isa 9:2) and "they will not hurt or destroy on all my holy mountain"

---

1. To watch this short, disturbing documentary, see www.meat.org.

(Isa 11:9). In this "already, but not yet" world, I try to make choices that reflect a reconciled creation, including a rejection of the violence and death necessary for the consumption of meat.

I am the firstborn child of recent Christian converts and was reared in a conservative, English-speaking, United-States-of-American, middle-class household. I was a longtime member of a conservative evangelical church and now belong to a community associated with the Brethren in Christ, but I was raised and still identify as "nondenominational." My theology and praxis continue to clarify with experience and insights from the Holy Spirit.

I believe that the Bible is an inspired word of God. Through the course of its narrative, scripture systematically reveals the nature and purpose of God's kingdom and clearly communicates God's plan to reconcile creation.

I believe that Jesus was God-enfleshed and that the Holy Spirit is God-in-us. God, Jesus, and the Holy Spirit are three names for God. When I worship, I typically think of God. When I meditate, I most often ask the Holy Spirit to come or the Lord Jesus to be my guide. When I seek to understand how best to live in the world, I try to follow Jesus's example. But whether I call the name of Jesus, Holy Spirit, or Lord God, I am reaching out to the one true God.

I believe that Jesus was crucified, died, and rose from death. I believe that on the cross, Jesus carried my sin and the sins of all the world, from all time. I believe Jesus is with me in struggle and pain and joy and frustration and love and celebration and birth and death and every experience in between.

I believe that God created the world and that it surely stretches far beyond human awareness. The eighth chapter of Romans tells us that all of creation will be reconciled to God. I believe that God is reflected in and glorified throughout creation. While God's original creation was perfect and peaceful, human sin marks the created world with struggle, suffering, and the joy of grace given freely. We struggle against a propensity for selfishness and sin, and we offer joyful thanksgiving for the grace that leads to reconciliation.

I believe that humans are made in the image of God and given a special responsibility for stewardship of the whole of creation. Human arrogance, among other sins, leads us to justify the horrific abuse of God's creation for our own selfish means.

I believe that through grace, created beings have the opportunity to be reconciled with one another, with creation, and with God. Grace is a gift from God, not earned or deserved. Grace is evidence of God's deep desire both to be in intimate relationship with us and to see us experience the joy of being in right relationship with the good creation and God. These questions of human nature, human destiny, and relationship among created beings have been foremost in my spiritual journey and have developed through reading, dialogue with other believers, and prayer.

I believe that God will continue to teach me, and am deeply aware of how much I have yet to learn. But I know that even when I am hardheaded and ill-willed, Jesus loves me deeply. Jesus also loves you deeply. And Jesus deeply loves the folks that you and I have a hard time loving. Like slow left-lane drivers and tailgaters.

1

Stealing Chickens in Austria

(IT WAS AN ACCIDENT, I SWEAR)

In 2004, I went to London to work with PETA UK. As a wannabe world traveler without two dimes to rub together, this was a dream come true. Close to the end of my time in London, I realized that I had spent far too many weekends wandering the same streets and watching DVDs by myself in a tiny rented flat, and I booked myself a ten-dollar weekend flight to Salzburg, Austria.

I arrived late, past dark, but managed, with the help of a Londoner in town for a dance-school audition, to find the hostel where we were both staying. There was a short walk after our bus ride, and though it was raining, we passed an outdoor sausage festival where a German band was playing the UB40 version of Elvis's "Can't Help Falling in Love," one of my all-time favorite songs. I took it as a sign that I was in God's hands, despite my travel jitters.

The next morning I set out to discover the city, found a vegetarian Indian restaurant, visited the free museums and Mahler's birthplace, and strolled on the north bank of the river. I wandered into the nineteenth-century evangelical *Christuskirche* to sit in silence and prayer, my back against the cool wooden pew, while the organist rehearsed for the next day's service. I had a deep sense of peace, of Christ next to me and accompanying my steps—perhaps the only way I could have managed a weekend trip to a foreign country alone.

On my second day in Salzburg, I took the obligatory *Sound of Music* tour (FYI, the gazebo is closed for those wishing to reenact a certain plucky dance scene, as some numbskull broke a leg attempting the feat) and navigated my way to a vegetarian festival that happened to be taking place in one of the city squares. In the category of "it really is a small world," I ran into an old acquaintance in a city five thousand miles from my home in a country where I barely spoke the language. As the festival came to a close, my friend—we'll call him Martin—let me know that a local grass-roots activist group was going to do an undercover investigation at a nearby chicken factory farm that evening. He asked if I wanted to come along.

The nature of undercover investigations is that they are stealthy. I am *not* stealthy. I am big and klutzy and bookish and a rule-follower. But I said yes, I want to come along on this investigation. When in Rome . . . or Salzburg.

So Martin and I went to a meeting where the plans for the evening were carefully hashed out. In German. More fancy German than I know, which is the high-school-discussion kind, mostly relating to the name of my uncle and the location of the nearest bathroom.

After what seemed like hours of talking, we finally all piled into cars and drove for miles and miles, out of the city and into the surrounding countryside. At this point, I started to question the wisdom of my tagging along on this adventure. What if I got separated from the group and was left to wander the Austrian countryside alone, in the dark (this was pre-iPhone, mind)? If we were caught, would I be deported? Would I be sent back to London, or to the U.S.? I was *terrified* that because I worked for PETA, I would drag the organization into my poor choice. When I realized that I was carrying my reflective messenger bag emblazoned with the PETA logo, I kicked myself a little harder.

Eventually, the drivers turned their lights off and pulled onto a gravel road. We parked in a clearing and walked back down a path to a giant ware-house filled with captive egg-laying hens. I told Martin I didn't want to go inside, pondering whether I'd claim he kidnapped me when the police caught and interrogated us under a harsh spotlight. Martin and a few of the others climbed through a vent and disappeared into the warehouse. I waited by stacks of crates. I knew what was inside—row upon row of cages, each packed with hens, stacked one on top of the other; the stink of am-monia, feces, dead and decaying birds would be overwhelming. Dead birds would be in cages with live birds, some of whose feet would have grown around the cage wires, since their movement was so restricted. I was afraid of being arrested, but I was also horrified to come face to face with the real-life suffering that, to this point, I'd only seen on video.

There was a steady rain falling and I was beginning to wonder if I should just cut my losses and start hiking back to Salzburg when Martin and a few of the others came back out of the warehouse. I asked him if we were done and was flooded with relief when he said yes. But my stomach turned into an iron ball when he followed with, "And now we are going to do the rescue!" He was elated. Despite the cold, I began sweating and my heart raced. I told him I wouldn't carry any crates. Couldn't. I was more concerned with my own well-being than with helping animals in desperate need of care.

The activists on the inside of the warehouse began carefully passing crates full of chirruping chickens out the open window. Each crate was carried down the driveway to a waiting van. Finally, the operation came to an end. I walked with two young activists carrying a final crate of chickens back to the clearing where we had parked. Halfway down the lane, we heard the crunch of tires on gravel and saw the stab of headlights in the distance. In the only agile moment of my lifetime, I dove over a fence alongside the road, into a ditch, and waited, panting and thinking many swear words to myself.

I heard the new vehicle continue past me, then stop a few yards ahead at our parked cars. A door opened and closed. I heard some words that I can only presume were "What the bleeding %*@ is this?" Some grunting followed, and I heard another door open, releasing a flood of soft chicken clucks into the still night air. An exclamation of surprise, probably some more German swearing, then the door closed and the clucks ceased. Another door opened, closed, and the wheels crunched on down the road, a little faster than before.

As soon as the visitor was out of sight, we bolted for the cars. I had no idea where Martin was and didn't want to stick around to find out. "Do you have keys?" I asked, now frantic. My new friends did have keys—to the van with all the rescued chickens. We piled in and drove away, not too fast, not too slow. Several miles down the road, we passed two police cars headed in the opposite direction and I begged the driver to let me out at the first possible stop. A gas station in a small town appeared to be open, so we pulled over and I jumped out. "You never saw me—I was never here!" were my parting words. I've always had a flair for the dramatic.

In the gas station, I splashed water on my face, straightened myself out, and tried to think of a reason, *any* reason, to be where I was (and just where was that?), in the middle of the night, alone. I came up with nothing, nada, zilch (did I mention that I am also a terrible liar?). When I came back out, by what I can only describe as God's grace, a taxi van was waiting to pick up two men who had been attending what they said was a birthday party in the back room of the garage. Glad that my mother would never know I got into a van with three strange men in the middle of the night in a foreign country, I showed the driver my (exorbitant) cash fare, hopped in the front seat, rolled down the window, chain-smoked on the hourlong drive back to the city (it was my year of poor choices, what can I say?), and thanked God for taking care of me.

I slept late the next day and that evening watched a film called *Blueprint* starring Franka Potente that made me sob in a tiny village theater. Despite the leftover adrenaline rush, I left Austria the following morning with a profound sense of peace.

I've struggled a bit over the years with what I participated in that night. On the one hand, I feel guilty that I helped commit a crime, albeit unintentionally. But despite my good-girl tendencies, I know how important undercover investigations and rescues are to exposing the truth of what goes on behind well-locked doors. The rescued hens were going to be taken to a veterinarian so that their illness and injuries could be documented, and then to a sanctuary where they would live the rest of their natural lives in peace. They would be able to feel the sun, breathe fresh air, and would never know the terror of a slaughterhouse. I didn't raise a finger to actually help those activists do the job that I believed they should be doing, because I was afraid for my personal comfort and reputation. Even though my convictions are strong, I was cowardly. It was my Peter moment.

Looking at the Word through an Animal Lens

Introduction to Part One

As evangelicals, our lives and decisions are shaped by scripture. But simply because we think "that's the way it's always been," we eat, wear, and use animals in ways that are not supported by the arc of the scriptural story, which starts and ends without violence and is infused with the anticipation and influence of the Prince of Peace.

In chapter 2, we'll take a good overview look at the creation account. You probably remember that in the first Genesis account of creation, God creates humans and land mammals on the sixth day, saying, "Let us make humankind in our image, according to our likeness; and let them have dominion over the fish of the sea, and over the birds of the air, and over the cattle, and over all the wild animals of the earth, and over every creeping thing that creeps upon the earth." God gives the instruction to "be fruitful and multiply" to birds and fish on the fifth day, and to humans on the sixth day. Here's what we overlook, though: to these humans made in God's likeness and given dominion over the earth—indeed, over *all* creation—God prescribes a vegan diet.

Chapter 3 will explore what it means to have dominion and to be made in the image of God. I'll point out that eating animals is one of many signs of the broken world after the fall, articulated in God's post-flood chat with Noah (Gen 9). Instead of God's perfect and balanced creation, this new world order is marked by fear and predation both between and among the species, though God clearly establishes a covenantal relationship with both human and animal creation, further evidenced by the inclusion of laws to protect animals in the Torah.

In chapter 4, we'll look at prophetic passages throughout the Hebrew Scriptures, which point to a future kingdom marked by peace both between and among the species. Joel 2:28 proclaims, "I will pour out my spirit on *all flesh*," while Hosea 2:18 visions a renewed covenant with "the wild animals, the birds of the air, and the creeping things of the ground . . . I will abolish the bow, the sword, and war from the land; and I will make you lie down in safety."

Chapters 5–7 are all about Jesus and his orientation to peace, which extends to all animals.

In chapter 8, we'll talk about how the book of Revelation continues the prophetic themes of the Hebrew Scriptures that point to the future reconciliation of God with all of creation, and of humans and animals with one another. Chapter 9 will address some of the commonly raised objections to the proposal that there is a biblical basis for Christian vegetarianism.

Now, let's get into it, shall we?

2

Creation

(OR, USING ANIMALS SAYS TO GOD, "I DON'T THINK
YOU GOT IT QUITE RIGHT IN GENESIS")

TAKE A GOOD, LONG, hard look at the first creation story set out in the first
chapter of Genesis. Don't skim because you've read it a million times, like
I used to. Here's the NRSV version of the bit I want us to focus on, in case
you don't want to get up to get your Bible:

> And God said, "Let the waters bring forth swarms of living crea-
> tures, and let birds fly above the earth across the dome of the sky."
> So God created the great sea monsters and every living creature
> that moves, of every kind, with which the waters swarm, and every
> winged bird of every kind. And God saw that it was good. God
> blessed them, saying, "Be fruitful and multiply and fill the waters
> in the seas, and let birds multiply on the earth." And there was
> evening and there was morning, the fifth day.
>
> And God said, "Let the earth bring forth living creatures of
> every kind: cattle and creeping things and wild animals of the
> earth of every kind." And it was so. God made the wild animals
> of the earth of every kind, and the cattle of every kind, and every-
> thing that creeps upon the ground of every kind. And God saw
> that it was good.
>
> Then God said, "Let us make humankind in our image, ac-
> cording to our likeness; and let them have dominion over the fish
> of the sea, and over the birds of the air, and over the cattle, and
> over all the wild animals of the earth, and over every creeping
> things that creeps upon the earth."
>
> So God created humankind in his image,

in the image of God he created them;
male and female he created them.

God blessed them, and God said to them, "Be fruitful and multiply, and fill the earth and subdue it; and have dominion over the fish of the sea and over the birds of the air and over every living thing that moves upon the earth." God said, "See, I have given you every plant yielding seed that is upon the face of all the earth, and every tree with seed in its fruit; you shall have them for food. And to every beast of the earth, and to every bird of the air, and to everything that creeps on the earth, everything that has the breath of life, I have given every green plant for food." And it was so. God saw everything that he had made, and indeed, it was very good. And there was evening and there was morning, the sixth day. (Gen 1:20–31)

What do you notice as you read? Read it again, slowly.

I read the Genesis story for years and years and years, even as a vegan animal person, and worried about the part where God gives humans dominion over animals. There it was, right at the start of the Bible—permission to use animals any which way we wanted to. Shoot.

But that's not actually what Genesis says. Not at all. Actually, it says kind of the opposite of that. First, God creates everything and everyone. It's all God's. But God shares the power to create and re-create. J. Richard Middleton points out that the sun is made to govern the day and the moon to govern the night, that God invites the earth and waters to produce life, and that all are made to reproduce their own kind. Our God "is generous with power, sharing it with creatures, that they might make their own contribution to the harmony and beauty of the world."[1] God's power in the creation story is a power of love, cooperation, and sustenance.

God announces that humankind is made in the image of God and humans are to have dominion over everything. And then right after that—right after God says, "Humans, you're made in my image and I'm giving you this whole thing to take care of"—God adds, "Here are all the plants to eat." Period. Not "here are the plants, they'll be a nice side dish to the dead animals and a hefty portion of starch." Just "eat plants." Moreover, God's original design also included plant-based diets for all animals. There was no killing—none. In the creation story, human dominion of the created world did not involve killing animals.

1. Middleton, *Liberating Image*, 288–89.

Human egocentricity has led to a host of sins, one of which is the break in human-animal relationships. Anthropocentric, rather than theocentric, interpretations of the creation story generally (and God's allowance for human dominion particularly) have led to gross abuses of creation by humans and have distorted the proper understanding of our place within God's creation. We've made the creation story about us instead of about God, and we've gone horribly wrong as a result.

God created this beautiful world in which birds were to fly across the dome of the sky (not be caged), fish were to swarm in the water, living creatures were to creep over the face of the earth, and humans were to be the caretakers of it all. Creation glorifies God. The creation story reminds us of God's awesome creative power, God's ability to bring order and beauty out of chaos, God's intimate attention to, and pleasure in, all creation. But we've decided the creation story is mostly about our being at the top of a food chain, the pinnacle of a cosmic pyramid, with every other created being there only to elevate and support the human. Our craving for flesh, our greed, is so strong that we have ignored God's command to eat plants and instead twisted scripture to suit our desires.

At the end of the sixth day, God saw the whole of the created earth. God saw the fish swimming and animals walking about and the humans taking care of it all. God saw animals and humans alike feasting on the abundant plants created for food, and God said that this was all very good. When we step back and look at the first Genesis creation story with a focus on God instead of on ourselves, we can begin to develop an alternate vision for the human's role in creation that does not inflate our position but still recognizes the *imago Dei*. With fresh eyes, we can then look around at the world today and ask, does this honor God's creation?

Mother pigs are kept in gestation and farrowing crates, unable to turn around, root for food, bathe, or display any of the characteristics that God gave them. They eat, sleep, and poop right in the same tiny area.

Chickens love to peck, hunt for food, dust-bathe, and play, but the vast majority of chickens are denied these simple pleasures.

Mother cows are separated from their babies within twelve hours of birth so that humans can have the milk meant for her calf.

Elephants in the wild walk hundreds of miles a day and travel in family packs. In zoos and circuses, they are separated from their families and confined up to twenty-four hours a day in boxcars or tiny enclosures.

Mice and rats are fastidiously clean, good mothers and fathers, and very intelligent. We treat them like unfeeling lab equipment instead of living, created beings.

Chimpanzees are incredibly intelligent and have learned to communicate with humans. We reward them with life in a cage, without so much as a toy to keep their keen minds occupied. We keep them in labs for decades, mutilating and torturing them until their bodies finally give out.

I'm not sure when we started to believe that because we were made in the image of God we had a license to mutilate, abuse, and kill. Wouldn't a better reflection of God and imitation of God's character be marked by love, mercy, and reconciliation?

3

What It Means to "Have Dominion"

"If God didn't want us to eat animals, why would they be made of meat?" "Humans didn't climb their way to the top of the food chain to eat vegetables!" "Animals are for people to use however they want." I was born and raised in a Christian home and took for granted that statements like these were true without questioning their ramifications on my relationship with God and the rest of God's creation. After I learned about violence-ridden standard agricultural practices and the inefficiency of producing animal foods for human consumption in the United States, along with the host of other ways humans have abused their position as stewards, I began to question these assumptions. In this chapter, I posit that a proper interpretation of dominion and the *imago Dei* is that humans are partners in a circle of all life, that all species depend on one another and are in God's care.

Dominion—Traditional Views

The first creation account in Genesis tells us that God said, "Let us make humankind in our image, according to our likeness; and let them have dominion over the fish of the sea, and over the birds of the air, and over the cattle, and over all the wild animals of the earth, and over every creeping thing that creeps upon the earth" (Gen 1:26). Reflecting centuries of Aristotelian thinking, humans have improperly viewed the *imago Dei* and dominion as rights rather than privileges. As a result, we have created a false hierarchy of dominant beings controlling and using "others" for our own gain.[1] Aquinas also viewed nonhuman animals in a utilitarian way—humans were not

1. Linzey, *Why Animal Suffering Matters*, 12.

connected in a holistic sense to creation. Instead, God's creation existed to serve humans, who were the divine image-bearers.[2] He argued against extending neighborly love to nonhuman animals because in his view, they "have no fellowship with man in the rational life."[3] But of course, basing the value of a life on the ability to reason is fraught with problems, to which those who work to protect the unborn, the developmentally delayed, and sufferers of dementia will attest.

The idea that animals are ours to use has been a widely accepted view throughout history. Vidler points to the frequent use of animals for human ends throughout the Bible as proof that their bodies are divinely granted for our means.[4] Calvin goes further, calling vegetarian diets "insupportable tyranny" and saying that they cause "atrocious injury" to God.[5] Others have used the assumption of difference as permission to act upon animals in any way they see fit, no matter how gruesome or cruel. Under the influence of Descartes and his teaching that animals were "thoughtless brutes," his supporters cut them open in city squares in order to study them, didn't bother to put them out of their misery, and equated their screams with the sounds of a machine that needed oiling. I really want to punch Descartes in the face, even though I try to be a nonviolent person. In these views, which have dominated Christian activity for centuries, humans are a species set above the rest, and it is our right and obligation to use the earth and its inhabitants to further human (and only human) self-interest.

Not every old European theologian got the creation story wrong. John Wesley points out that the humans who were originally granted dominion over creation were far more impressive than the broken ones who emerged from the ark. Wesley preached that Adam was "the supreme perfection of man . . . continually seeing, and loving, and obeying the Father of the spirits of all flesh . . . To *this* creature, endued with all these excellent faculties, thus qualified for his high charge, God said, 'Have thou dominion.'"[6] Unlike Calvin's claim that to refrain from eating meat is "tyranny," Wesley argued that humans have so corrupted the original meaning of dominion that they

---

2. Linzey, *Animal Theology*, 18.

3. Ibid., 14.

4. Vidler, "Animals," cited in Linzey and Regan, *Animals and Christianity*, 197–98.

5. Calvin, *Commentaries on the First Book of Moses*, cited in Linzey and Regan, *Animals and Christianity*, 200.

6. Wesley, "Sermon LXV: The General Deliverance," in *Sermons on Several Occasions*, 254.

have become tyrants themselves: "The human shark, without any such necessity, torments [animals] of his own free choice: and, perhaps, continues
their lingering pain, till, after months or years, death signs their release."[7]

Regardless of whether or not the human is a tyrant for eating flesh
or a tyrant for refraining from animal flesh, in this framework, humans
stand between God and animals. From the perspective of both Calvin and
Wesley, the only value that animals provide creation is their use to humans.
Though the self-serving view has been popular, it is unbiblical.

Typically, both the subject and object of the Hebrew word translated
in the Genesis creation story as "dominion" (רָדָה, *rdh*) are human, and the
word frequently refers to the actions of a king: neither is the case in Genesis
1:26.[8] Further, while violence and force are frequently associated with the
use of *rdh* in the Hebrew Scriptures, in Genesis 1:26 and 28, a slightly different interpretation is required, precisely because we view the verb through
the lens of being made in the image of God. God deals mercifully with us,
evidenced over and over again both in the Bible and in history. God, who
is all-powerful, deals with our ineptitude with overwhelming kindness and
sacrifice . . . and we reflect that by engaging in the wholesale slaughter and
destruction of other created beings. Something is terribly amiss.

What if we thought about dominion here as a blessing to bless, instead
of violently suppress?[9] And what if we consider that this blessing is followed
immediately by a prescription for a plant-based diet? "The right to kill animals is excluded from the lordship of human beings over them . . . Human
lordship on earth is the lordship exercised by a tenant on God's behalf. It
means stewardship over the earth, for God."[10] When God granted dominion over the new creation and told human creatures to be its stewards, God
did not mean that we could eat animals. This is made so very clear by the
very next declaration: that animals and humans alike are to eat only plants.

Creation receives its value not from the actions of humans but directly
from God. As a result, the value of nonhuman creation to humans is un-
related to its value to God, and we must begin to realize that since animals
have value to God apart from their use to us, it is out of step with our role as
protector and caretaker to exercise tyranny and absolute power (the power
of life and death) over animals, particularly if granting or taking life has

7. Ibid., 257.

8. Zobel, "רָדָה," 331.

9 Ibid., 335.

10. Moltmann, *Creating a Just Future*, 224.

nothing whatsoever to do with the animals' own welfare and serves only to satisfy our greed or appetite. Absolute power and the wielding of absolute power rests solely in God's hands.[11]

When coupled with the *imago Dei*, dominion must be exercised as God's caring hand, not an iron fist. "The task of 'dominion' does not have to do with exploitation and abuse. It has to do with securing the well-being of every other creature and bringing the promise of each to full fruition."[12] Some traditional interpretations of *imago Dei* and the task of dominion have contributed to a dangerous trend among Euro-Western contemporary Christians to trample on nonhuman creation and deny or dismiss the disastrous consequences of humancentric interpretations of the creation story, including the devastating impact of environmental destruction on the world's most impoverished human inhabitants.[13] Even critiques calling for humans to exercise restraint and responsibility in their dealings with creation order the creation story around humans—human rights, human responsibilities, human relationships.

How did this happen? One Jewish theologian points to translation choices as the root of historical decisions about the role of animals in relation to human creation:

> As the offspring of God's word and the earth's fertile receptiveness to God's command, animals are described as "living souls" or "living beings" (*nephesh*). The exact same term is used in Genesis to describe human beings, and thus implies a profound kinship, making human-animal ontological continuity explicit. Other Hebrew biblical terminology reflects this unity . . . the phrase "spirit of life" (*ruach hayyim*) can indicate both animals and humans, as can the word "flesh" (*basar*) . . . In a similar manner, the expression "all flesh" (*kol basar*) can mean "all living creatures, animal as well as human."[14]

What the faithful Christian is left to do, then, is refrain from using an argument in favor of human worth in order to devalue other God-created beings.[15] In other words, God has enough love for every being. Yes, every being.

---

11. Linzey, *Christianity and the Rights of Animals*, 25–26.

12. Brueggemann, *Genesis*, 32.

13. Woodley, *Shalom*, 57.

14. Moritz, "Animals and the Image of God," 135.

15. Linzey, *Christianity and the Rights of Animals*, 75–76.

Dominion—Contemporary Views

Some modern theologies attempt to counter the traditional view of dominion and forward a more sustainable theology of humanity in creation by calling for human stewardship of creation, perhaps to make consideration for nonhuman interests more palatable. It is nice to be needed, after all. Biblical commentator R. R. Reno says that the exercise of dominion allows things to "flourish according to their proper purposes."[16] Reno also claims that "to govern and be governed is a crucial way in which humans differ from animals,"[17] a statement that betrays a lack of understanding of animal behavior (think about pecking order, pack behavior, etc.).

Let's problematize this notion of stewardship. There is an implicit and dangerous hierarchy in the idea of stewardship as it is presented today, a privileging of human animals over nonhuman ones. Miller, for instance, argues that nonhuman animals do not have a choice to be in relationship with God, that what sets humans apart is our ability, our freedom, to choose to accept or decline the responsibility God has bestowed on us. As a result, human-to-human relationships have an inherent mutuality of which human-animal relationships are not capable. Our relational nature rightly includes relations with nonhuman creation, though humans carry the burden of moral responsibility for our relationships with nonhuman created beings.[18] Miller here is attempting to widen the circle of human compassion, but his model still ultimately relies on a humancentric reading of the Genesis creation story.

Though eco-feminist theologian Sallie McFague also argues for a more holistic and responsible view of humans in creation, including a strong interdependence, her analysis of the nature of the *imago Dei* also reflects a built-in hierarchical view of humans. McFague's model of God as Mother and analogy of humans as co-creators in the garden of creation attempts to subvert the traditional paternocentric theology, but still relies on humans as special administrators of ecological balance.[19] The challenge of McFague's model is that it may be difficult to understand oneself and other humans as caretakers, as the only conscienticized beings, the only

---

16. Reno, *Genesis*, 54.

17. Ibid., 55.

18. Miller, "Responsible Relationship," 335–39.

19. McFague, *Models of God*, 120.

beings aware of our cultural, historical, and physical place, and still manage to reject hierarchies that ultimately cause a superiority complex.[20]

McFague argues that human dependence on nonhuman creation actually makes us more vulnerable.[21] McFague wants humans to understand how dependent they are on nonhuman creation, which is a noble sentiment, but tell a baby pig being slammed to death on the floor of a factory farm, or a downed cow dragged into the slaughterhouse at the end of a chain, strung up by a leg and sliced from stem to stern, that the human hands perpetrating this violence are "vulnerable." These beings are not empowered by such a hollow declaration.

Theological arguments made from a Native-American perspective provide some relief from the dependence on hierarchy and human-focused accounts of creation. Important to a Native American theological anthropology is the understanding of reciprocity. Nonhuman creation is not off-limits for human consumption and use, but such use must be carefully measured. When use requires harm (as in hunting, or cutting plants), the sacrifice must be honored by thoughtful preparation and a reciprocal offering.[22] Unlike McFague, the worldview here is represented not by a ladder of hierarchy or a pyramid of privilege but a circle, in which human and nonhuman creatures are "co-equal participants in the circle standing neither above nor below anything else in God's Creation. There is no hierarchy in our cultural context, even of species, because the circle has no beginning or ending."[23]

Humans apart from God are nothing, according to Karl Barth.[24] Native American theologians would add that humans apart from the whole of God's creation are as much at risk as those cut off from God.[25] While Europeans and many Christians view themselves as outsiders in relation to creation, looking back on "Creation" as a finite divine act or standing over it to observe the results, the Native American intellectual tradition sees the created world as "alive and sentient as human beings are . . . we are related

---

20. Ibid., 77.

21. McFague, *Body of God*, 106.

22. Kidwell et al., *Native American Theology*, 41–42.

23. Ibid., 50. George Tinker is primarily responsible for the chapter in which I found this quote.

24. Barth, *Church Dogmatics* III/2, 68.

25. Kidwell et al., *Native American Theology*, 40.

to all of these sentient persons in creation."[26] The understanding of "persons" here is not reserved for a specific species, genus, family, or phylum of beings, but rather for every work of God's hand, every member of the created kingdom, including those we have classified as plants and animals. Thus, a sacred ritual performed before war is virtually identical to the one performed by the community before embarking on a buffalo hunt.[27]

Holistic Vision of the Human's Role in Creation

Animals were not created for human ends, but for God's. All of creation, from the tallest tree to the smallest insect, belongs to the Creator. "Coming in last place [in the creation story] should give us all pause for creaturely humility. We should realize that everything created was not made primarily for human happiness. Obviously, creation was enjoyed prior to our arrival."[28] Yet we humans have placed ourselves at the center of the creation story. We remove ourselves from the symbiotic harmony of God's creation.[29] For many years, I intentionally alienated myself from the truth about where animal foods came from in order to avoid feeling guilty about eating them.

When we embrace God's commands in Genesis, and if we keep these commands in mind as we consider the whole biblical narrative, we can begin to develop an alternate vision for the human's role in creation that does not rely on hierarchy but still recognizes the *imago Dei*. Humans are not little gods on earth. We are created "to be his image,"[30] a reality only fully realized in and through the person of Christ, our best understanding of being made in the image of God. And when we look at Jesus, we see mercy on a radical level. We see love and sacrifice. We see service.

Our dominion in creation is not one of paternalistic overseers (uncomfortably reminiscent of justifications for slavery), or even of siblings, but of servants. Christ calls us to love and to serve, and it is only through Christ that we are able to love and serve. But we do not love only our family, our friends. We do not love only our neighbors. We do not love only those who look like us, who share our political views, or who love us in return. Christ calls us to love our enemies. Christ calls us to love those we do not

26. Ibid., 35.
27. Ibid., 43.
28. Woodley, *Shalom*, 53.
29. Ibid., 51.
30. Moltmann, *God in Creation*, 218.

understand and do not appreciate. Christ calls us to love the leper. In our time, that must include the furry, the finned, and the feathered. In loving and serving others throughout the whole of the created community, we love and serve Christ.[31]

31. Largen, "Christian Rationale," 155.

4

The Prophets

I LOVE THE PROPHETS. They're full of righteous anger. They don't pull punches. They have big visions and get super frustrated when the Israelites just can't seem to get their collective act together. Prophets are demanding. They have high standards and don't accept less. When we read the prophets, we get an inkling of what is to come. We are instructed to live lives marked by love, justice, mercy, stewardship, peacemaking, and nonviolence. But what we do to animals today doesn't match those virtues we seek to embody. Prophets are looking around and ahead. They're looking at how the people of God are living in their current context, calling them out on their failures, and letting them know that something better is coming. But there's urgency here. A sense that, no, really y'all, we need to be paying attention to these problems because this is *not* how God ordered things.

One of the consistent themes in the prophetic books is that the reign of God (more on that in chapter 8) is marked by the reconciliation of creation to Creator. It's marked by the shalom, peace, between all beings.

> The wolf shall live with the lamb, the leopard shall lie down with the kid, the calf and the lion and the fatling together, and a little child shall lead them. The cow and the bear shall graze, their young shall lie down together; and the lion shall eat straw like the ox. The nursing child shall play over the hole of the asp, and the weaned child shall put its hand on the adder's den. They will not hurt or destroy on all my holy mountain; for the earth will be full of the knowledge of the Lord as the waters cover the sea. On that day the root of Jesse shall stand as a signal to the peoples; the nations shall inquire of him, and his dwelling shall be glorious. (Isa 11:6–10)

Think of it. Think of a world where predator and prey relate to each other in a new, reconciled way. Think of a world with *no human violence, and no animal violence, either.* None. We're in the garden of Eden again. The knowledge of good and evil is withered up and gone because the world is full of the knowledge of the Lord and the Lord is good. The Lord is perfect. The Lord is right. The Lord is healing. The Lord is creation. The Lord is wholeness. The Lord is goodness. The Lord is mercy. The Lord is forgiveness. The Lord is compassion. The Lord is salvation. The Lord is beauty. The Lord is love.

This world that Isaiah promises to us is imminent. It's not a far-off, someday, too-bad-the-world's-so-sad eventuality. The root of Jesse, Jesus, has already come. Jesus brought the possibility of this perfect world to us two thousand years ago in Palestine. Jesus incarnated the reign of God on earth, and Jesus told us to go out and be like our Master, the God of love, the God of mercy, justice, service, sacrifice, and more. Jesus didn't tell us to sit tight and wait on being sucked up into heaven when we die. Jesus called us to live into the reign of God *now*. In our lives. In our lifetime.

And what does that mean? Love our neighbor. Love our enemy. And try our sinful best not to hurt or destroy one another, but rather to foster a world where wolves and lambs and children play together and where there are no more predators and no more prey.

You know who has some ability to bring about this world? We humans do. We choose violence. We choose harm. We choose to cover our ears and sing "lalalalalala" when we don't want to hear how our actions cause gross abuse and gruesome death. True, wolves still hunt sheep and lions still eat flesh. But does that give us license to kill? No. The world may not be perfect, and we may not be able to do much to stem the tide of pain and injury, but most of us can make more compassionate choices each day. And for now, those compassionate choices may be all we can do to reflect the kingdom to come.

> I am the LORD, your Holy one, the Creator of Israel, your King. Thus says the LORD, who makes a way in the sea, a path in the mighty waters, who brings out chariot and horse, army and warrior; they lie down, they cannot rise, they are extinguished, quenched like a wick: Do not remember the former things, or consider the things of old. I am about to do a new thing; now it springs forth, do you not perceive it? I will make a way in the wilderness and rivers in the desert. The wild animals will honor me, the jackals and the ostriches; for I give water in the wilderness, rivers in the desert,

to give drink to my chosen people, the people whom I formed for myself so that they might declare my praise. (Isa 43:15–21)

Let's take a detour to the Psalms, where we read, "Your steadfast love, O LORD, extends to the heavens, your faithfulness to the clouds. Your righteousness is like the mighty mountains, your judgments are like the great deep; you save humans and animals alike, O LORD" (Ps 36:5–6) We're not the only beings who can honor God. Yet we systematically breed, mutilate, and kill billions upon billions of creatures each year. How vain. How utterly vain.

For I am about to create new heavens and a new earth; the former things shall not be remembered or come to mind. But be glad and rejoice forever in what I am creating; for I am about to create Jerusalem as a joy, and its people as a delight. I will rejoice in Jerusalem, and delight in my people; no more shall the sound of weeping be heard in it, or the cry of distress. No more shall there be in it an infant that lives but a few days, or an old person who does not live out a lifetime; for one who dies at a hundred years will be considered a youth, and one who falls short of a hundred will be considered accursed. They shall build houses and inhabit them; they shall plant vineyards and eat their fruit. They shall not build and another inhabit; they shall not plant and another eat; for like the days of a tree shall the days of my people be, and my chosen shall long enjoy the work of their hands. They shall not labor in vain, or bear children for calamity; for they shall be offspring blessed by the LORD—and their descendants as well. Before they call I will answer, while they are yet speaking I will hear. The wolf and the lamb shall feed together, the lion shall eat straw like the ox; but the serpent—its food shall be dust! They shall not hurt or destroy on all my holy mountain, says the LORD. (Isa 65:17–25)

Two main takeaways: one, the whole "wolf and lamb shall feed together" wasn't just an analogy. They really mean it. And two, even the serpent gets food. It gets even clearer in chapter 66:

Thus says the LORD: Heaven is my throne and the earth is my footstool; what is the house that you would build for me, and what is my resting place? All these things my hand has made, and so all these things are mine, says the LORD. But this is the one to whom I will look, to the humble and contrite in spirit, who trembles at my word. Whoever slaughters an ox is like one who kills a human being; whoever sacrifices a lamb, like one who breaks a dog's neck; whoever presents a grain offering, like one who offers swine's blood; whoever makes a memorial offering of frankincense, like one who blesses an idol. These have chosen their own ways, and in their abominations they take delight. (Isa 66:1–3)

The whole earth is the Lord's. Think of it as a rental house. Instead of treating it with respect and care, we're throwing wild parties and trashing the place every weekend. And then we're going to try to get our security deposit back?

While we're in the neighborhood, take a quick peek at Daniel 1:12–21. It's the story of how Daniel and his buddies eat a vegan diet for ten days and are a lot healthier than the king's men.

In Hosea, we read about a land in which "there is no faithfulness or loyalty, and no knowledge of God" (4:1). Doesn't sound good. What does that look like? "Swearing, lying, and murder, and stealing and adultery break out; bloodshed follows bloodshed" (4:2). So what happens? "Therefore the land mourns, and all who live in it languish; together with the wild animals and the birds of the air, even the fish of the sea are perishing" (4:3). Why? Because humans aren't removed from the created world, we are one piece of it. And bloodshed follows bloodshed, regardless of species.

Joel 2 provides some interesting images. God urges animals of the field not to fear because their pastures are green and lush, trees are bearing fruit and the vines are heavy (v. 22). God then goes on to tell the children of God to be glad, because their storehouses of grain will be full, and their vats will overflow with wine and oil. They are assured that they will eat and be satisfied, and never again be ashamed (vv. 23–27). Then God says, "I will pour out my spirit on *all flesh* . . ." (v. 28). I'm thinking about what this all means and wonder if the animals of the field can take a relaxing breath because the joyous, satisfied people won't be feasting on their flesh anymore. After the flood, God stated that fear and dread would be on every living creature, since not one of them was safe from the human plate. Here, we have the reverse of that—a release of living creatures from lives of fear, because the storehouses of humans are filled with the Eden diet of plants. And perhaps, as it was in Narnia, the animals will speak to us again.

Micah, too, employs imagery of a world without fear: "They shall beat their swords into plowshares, and their spears into pruning hooks . . . they shall sit under their own vines and under their own fig trees, and no one shall make them afraid" (4:3–4). Further, we're told in verse 8 that "the former dominion shall come, the sovereignty of daughter Jerusalem." Is it likely that the dominion and sovereignty of which the prophet speaks is intended to speak encouragement to a nation that had been in profound exile? Yes. But consider applying the gift of that restoration to a renewed understanding of human dominion. God releases the Israelites from captivity and promises to restore them to a life of shalom, a life that doesn't require weapons and that is not marked by fear. What if we did the same? What if we committed to living lives and enacting policies that didn't strike fear in the hearts of our fellow created beings, both human and nonhuman? What if we, now, beat our swords into plowshares and feasted on the abundance of God's earth without shedding blood? In fact, later in Micah, we're encouraged to do just that:

> "With what shall I come before the LORD, and bow myself before God on high? Shall I come before him with burnt offerings, with calves a year old? Will the LORD be pleased with thousands of rams, with ten thousands of rivers of oil? Shall I give my firstborn for my transgression, the fruit of my body for the sin of my soul?" He has told you, O mortal, what is good; and what does the LORD require of you but to do justice, and to love kindness, and to walk humbly with your God? (Mic 6:6–8)

Do justice. Love kindness. Walk humbly. Do justice. Love kindness. Walk humbly. Sound like someone we know?

5

Jesus, the Prince of Peace

I CAME OF AGE in the WWJD era. We had bracelets and bumper stickers and T-shirts. And after we exhausted the marketing possibilities of what Jesus would do, we started to ask what Jesus would drive and what Jesus would eat. There are people who argue that Jesus might have been a vegetarian. I am not one of those people. Though I admit that the image of Jesus gnawing on flesh doesn't jibe with my Christology, I don't want to argue about it. I don't think that whether Jesus ate meat two thousand years ago is the most important question for Christians to ask today, just as I don't think that it's a good use of time or resources to speculate on whether or not Jesus would drive a Humvee with a freshly killed deer strapped to the top through a KFC drive thru to get a snack on the way to his McMansion where he'd spend the afternoon playing *Call of Duty* and drinking beer. Jesus's cultural context was a lot different than mine. Would Jesus use an iPhone? Have a Facebook account? Would Jesus's disciples follow him on Twitter? God only knows.

If we embrace the idea that following Jesus means much more than guaranteeing our own personal escape from eternal damnation, if we understand that the good news of Christ speaks healing not only into our own sick souls but also into sick structures, if we believe that Jesus's life is the foundation on which the reign of God will be built, we have to ask ourselves how *we* Jesus followers can most faithfully embody the virtues and values that Jesus called us to. The scriptures give us so much rich material to work with, and we already ignore the vast majority of that. So the question to ask isn't what Jesus would do or drive or eat today, but what *we* should do or drive or eat based on what we understand about Jesus. To make these decisions well, we must understand both Christ and christological power.

So who is this Jesus? Jesus is God enfleshed, fully God and fully human, born a defenseless baby into poverty, in the midst of a violent military occupation, to a virgin and a carpenter, the product of a storied genealogy that included prostitutes (Rahab), foreigners (Ruth), rejects (Tamar), and the occasional king. As an infant, Jesus was thrust into the life of a refugee, fleeing Herod's fear-induced genocide of Hebrew boys. As an adult, Jesus's message was one of radical inclusion. Being the product of the aforementioned prostitutes, foreigners, rejects, and kings, it shouldn't have been *that* surprising that Jesus regularly touched the untouchable, returned dignity to those from whom it had been stripped, and protected not only those whom the world sought to harm but also the very people complicit in his crucifixion.

Jesus's Sermon on the Mount outlines what it means to be a faithful believer, including prioritizing relationships and reconciliation over legalism and rule following.[1] During Jesus's ministry years, he was challenged by the religious and political elites. After only a few years of formal ministry, he was killed in a way designed to maximize his humiliation and terrify others into submission. Jesus's life inaugurated the reign of God, though that reign has not yet been fully realized. In this "already, but not yet" tension, Jesus's followers are called to prayerfully live into a world "on earth, as it is in heaven."

What does that mean for our behavior toward nonhuman creation? The Genesis reality of humans made in the image of God was fully realized in and through the person of Christ. But we don't think that Palestinian men or carpenters are more Godlike because they share those specific attributes with Christ. Christ is the Word become *flesh*. Christ wasn't "en-manned," Christ was "incarnate"—enfleshed in solidarity with all creatures.[2] That kind of Jesus move is so typical of a Christ who turns ideas of power and faithfulness on their heads, showing his followers incredible new ways to be in relationship both with God and with the rest of God's created world.

---

1. I'm indebted to the late Glen Stassen and to David Gushee for their book *Kingdom Ethics*.

2. Clough, *On Animals*, 83–86. Clough points out that the author of the Johannine Gospel uses the Greek word *sarx* ("flesh") to talk about the incarnation of the Word. *Sarx* is related to the Hebrew word *basar*, used frequently in the Hebrew Scriptures to refer to all living creatures. So, when we say that Jesus was God "incarnate," we're not saying that God was only human, but that God was a "fleshly creature." Clough's systematic theology of animals (the first ever published!) is pricey but a must-read for any serious scholar of animal theology.

Jesus wasn't the sort of king that we expected to see. But the God who acquiesced in 1 Samuel and gave the Israelites a human king did a new thing in Jesus. This King of kings was seen by the dominant powers as weak and stupid. They failed to understand God's wisdom and strength.[3]

You see, there's strength in weakness. There's strength in vulnerability. And I'm not romanticizing suffering or anything white-privilegey like that. I'm saying that Jesus showed both the powerful and powerless how to live in the image of God and how to show God to one another. To those who were oppressed and marginalized, he gave a voice, a name, and a place at the table. To those who were abusive and powerful, he gave a voice, a name, and a place at the table. Andy Crouch writes that Jesus is "completely at home with power. What he is entirely indifferent to, indeed averse to, are the privilege, status, and prerequisites that preoccupy powerful people who have forgotten what power is for."[4]

Andrew Linzey suggests that christological power is "the power to serve."[5] I propose that a strong Christology, a confident understanding of who Jesus is and how Jesus calls us to live, doesn't allow for the kinds of abuses and uses that we see in our modern treatment of nonhuman creation. We can look back at Genesis here, in which our role as caretakers did not include killing animals. What would Jesus say to humans who look at animals as inanimate objects to be used for their pleasure and then justify their behavior by saying, "We're made in the image of God"?

Power exercised christologically "makes no appeal to equality. The obligation is always and everywhere on the 'higher' to sacrifice for the 'lower'; for the strong, powerful, and rich to give to those who are vulnerable, poor, or powerless."[6] Jesus came to us as a humble servant (cf. Mark 10:45; John 13:1–20; Acts 3:13; Phil 2:5–9). Just before he was crucified, Jesus reminded the disciples that what we do to the "least of these" we do

3. Card, "God's Own Fool," lines 1–16. This song was the first time I thought of Jesus as subversive. It's a great song.

4. Crouch, "It's Time to Talk about Power," 35. Of course, I recognize the irony in saying, "Hey, I'm not being white privilegey," and then quoting a privileged white man to talk about Jesus and power. We'll talk a lot more about Jesus through the lens of those who are oppressed in Part Three. But the point here is the same: Jesus turned what we thought we knew about power upside down, shook it out, and made something new out of the junk that fell out of its pockets. I'm glad that more and more Jesus-following white men are saying that, and I hope it means the church starts to do a better job at being the church.

5. Linzey, Why Animal Suffering Matters, 15.

6. Linzey, Animal Theology, 32.

to him (Matt 25:40). We are called to serve, whether or not we have worldly power. "Power is not given to benefit those who hold it. It is given for the flourishing of individuals, people, and the cosmos itself. Power's right use is especially important for the flourishing of the vulnerable . . . Power is not the opposite of servanthood. Rather, servanthood, ensuring the flourishing of others, is the very purpose of power."[7]

Christological power is shared power. Paul says it beautifully in Philippians 2:5–8: "Let the same mind be in you that was in Christ Jesus, who, though he was in the form of God, did not regard equality with God as something to be exploited, but emptied himself, taking the form of a slave, being born in human likeness . . . He humbled himself." God made humans in the image of God, then took on the likeness of humans to show us how it should be done, how to live and be and relate and even how to die in a broken world. And what did that look like? Military conquest? Corporate success? Riches beyond measure? Status and prestige? Climbing some invisible ladder, stepping on top of those who couldn't climb as fast or high? Power looked like service, relationships, healing, forgiveness, and humility. Walter Brueggeman says that "the key mark of Jesus in the image/form of God is that he did not grasp after equality with God but became obedient. God is the one who does not grasp. And human persons in his image are those who do not grasp. Grasping power cannot create. Grasping power cannot enhance creation . . . Grasping brings death."[8] Or, as my dad puts it, "Jesus died with His hands open to the world."

Grasping does bring death, and not only death to one another. Death to the world. The human propensity to grasp for power, generation after generation, has led to a catastrophic climate crisis. Grasping for power has left the majority of the world in desolate poverty. Grasping for power has decimated untold numbers of species of plants and animals, created by God, destroyed by humans. The scriptures are jam-packed with illustrations of Jesus's ethic of inclusion, protection, and care.

Jesus loved the unlovable. In first-century Palestine, the unlovable were women, children, sick people, poor people, Roman soldiers, zealots, lepers, the blind, the outcast, prostitutes, lying and arrogant men. Who are the unlovable today? It's easy to look back and see who needed love, protection, and inclusion then, but who needs that today? I know many amazing people working to love, protect, and include immigrants, former sex-trade

7. Crouch, "It's Time to Talk about Power," 35.

8. Brueggeman, *Genesis*, 34.

workers, the impoverished or imprisoned, children, and many others who have been systematically oppressed by those grasping for power.

Nonhuman creation needs advocates, too. And whether or not we know it, those of us who speak up on behalf of animals are taking our cues from the God who was enfleshed, who sought to include the misunderstood and marginalized, who broke race, class, and gender barriers in order to love and redeem a whole earth full of the glory of God.

$$6$$

I Think Jesus Dug Birds, Too

JESUS DIDN'T TALK MUCH about animal rights *per se*. I hope he would have a lot to say these days to folks who treat the created earth like it's their personal resource bank, but the scripture doesn't record any explicit exhortations from Jesus along the lines of "Blessed are the vegan, for they shall receive much tofu." Then again, first-century Palestine wasn't exactly teeming with factory farms.

> Are not five sparrows sold for two pennies? Yet not one of them is forgotten in God's sight. But even the hairs of your head are all counted. Do not be afraid; you are of more value than many sparrows. (Luke 12:6–7)

What if being more valuable than a sparrow didn't mean you had free license to go sparrow hunting, but that you were probably then *more responsible* to serve sparrows, who are perceived as having *less value*?

While so many of Jesus's teachings can be easily applied to today's contexts, simply because the nature of being human and broken hasn't changed all that much in two thousand years, Jesus's followers know that, in modern contexts, we are often faced with situations that the Bible doesn't speak to directly. So, we develop a normative framework—we look at the scriptures to determine how we should order our steps, what truths guide our decision-making, how the application of Jesus's teachings in the first century *can* be applied today, even if those applications are not spelled out in the gospels.[1]

---

1. I really like Ron Sider's way of developing a biblical analysis for contemporary social issues, from which this idea of a normative framework is taken. See especially his *Just Generosity*.

> "Jerusalem, Jerusalem, the city that kills the prophets and stones those who are sent to it! How often have I desired to gather your children together as a hen gathers her brood under her wings, and you were not willing!" (Luke 13:34)

When Jesus uses chickens and sparrows and other birds to talk about love, I wonder if it's a call to stretch our compassion a little further than we've been comfortable with before. Because isn't the kingdom of God about allowing the Holy Spirit to move us from what is to what ought to be? God is love. And if we are to reflect God, our behavior must be loving.

> He also said, "With what can we compare the kingdom of God, or what parable will we use for it? It is like a mustard seed, which, when sown upon the ground, is the smallest of all the seeds on earth; yet when it is sown it grows up and becomes the greatest of all shrubs, and puts forth large branches, so that the birds of the air can make nests in its shade." (Mark 4:30–32)

Check it out. Jesus is letting us know that a thriving, restored, flourishing creation is coming and that birds will have a pretty sweet home there.

—— 7 ——

The Good Samaritan:
Animals as Neighbors

I've BEEN AN ACTIVIST since I was old enough to walk. For most of my life, my passion was poured into the pro-life movement. None of my Christian friends and family ever questioned whether or not the defenseless beings I was working to protect needed or deserved my help. I was speaking up for the voiceless, and that was a Good Thing. Eventually, I started to advocate for animals as a full-time job. I didn't stop loving Jesus. I didn't stop advocating for peace and life for humans everywhere. I just started to advocate for nonhuman animals, too. And when that started, so did the pushback: "Aren't there other things that are more important?" "What about the starving kids in Africa?" "Shouldn't you work to solve human problems first?" "What, are you going to step over a homeless dude and feed his dog?"

I understand the concern. One of my closest friends spent a lot of time in foster homes as a teenager. He and houses full of kids without families would be watching TV and hear the familiar Sarah McLachlan refrain as pictures of abused and homeless dogs and cats flashed across the screen. He still gets pretty fired up at the memory and says he'll be happy to start worrying about homeless dogs and cats as soon as people start airing commercials for homeless kids. I totally get it. But here's the thing—if God is calling you to reduce homelessness, dig wells in Africa, fight poverty, minister to the dying, stop sex trafficking, fix a broken education system, reduce gun violence, foster world peace or racial reconciliation, or any other Really Godly Use of Time, you can do any of that and simultaneously help stop cruelty to animals. One vegetarian saves more than one hundred lives a year. Period. No protesting, no sacrifices of the tract-handing-out, quitting-of-full-time-job kind required. Helping animals and helping people are not mutually exclusive propositions. In fact, they are closely linked.

In chapter 5, we talked about how a strong Christology—taking seriously our call to be Christlike—actually supports our abstention from participating in cruelty, including cruelty to animals. When we seek to emulate Christ, the enfleshed God, we seek lives of service, of compassion, of justice, of mercy, of love.

One striking example of the power of service is in the story of the Good Samaritan (Luke 10:25–37). When the story begins, Jesus is teaching a small crowd. A lawyer asks Jesus how he can inherit eternal life. We're told the man is testing Jesus, who responds as a teacher does, with a question: "What is written in the law?" The lawyer answers, "You shall love the Lord your God with all your heart, and with all your soul, and with all your strength, and with all your mind, and your neighbor as yourself." Jesus commends him, but the lawyer pushes back: "And who is my neighbor?" So, Jesus tells the story of a man who travelled a dangerous road and was overcome by robbers. A priest and a Levite pass him but a Samaritan stops, is moved with compassion, and saves him from certain death. Jesus asks the lawyer which of the three was a neighbor. The lawyer answers, "The one who showed him mercy," and Jesus instructs his listener, "Go and do likewise." In this story, the hero is the person who crosses the road and saves the life of another—and he is a Samaritan: a no-class, unclean, cast-out, bottom-of-the-barrel foreigner.

Through the lens of this parable, through the lens of Jesus, "neighbor" is not only social location but also action, and specifically love in action. Using a Samaritan to illustrate neighborly love was a game changer in first-century Palestine. It was astounding to think that a lowly Samaritan could demonstrate love, and unthinkable to cross the rigid cultural boundaries that prohibited showing mercy or friendship to this particular "other." Perhaps it is just as astounding to consider crossing rigid species boundaries to extend mercy and friendship to nonhuman animals. But consider that with each passing era, humans acknowledge past grievous injuries (slavery, child labor, the subjugation of women, the wanton abuse of natural resources) and work to heal them. It is not up to us to decide which "others" we should love as we are loved. Instead, Jesus tells us that we are to love those we see with a need we can meet.

The parable of the Good Samaritan is not the only place Jesus makes the outrageous admonition to love and care for the unlovable other (remember that crazy call to "love your enemies"?). We are to respond in love to those who persecute us, who want to murder our families and us. How much more is our obligation to respond in love to the vulnerable creatures God has placed in the world alongside us? Daniel Miller points out that "granting neighborly love to animals does not lead to a diminishment of the Christian's capacity to love human neighbors."[1] Indeed, doesn't our capacity for communion with God and neighbor demand from us a praxis of care or companionship, rather than cruelty?

Jesus didn't tell us to love sometimes and hate at other times. Jesus didn't tell us to be merciful when it was convenient and to turn a blind eye when we felt uncomfortable. Jesus didn't tell us to categorize and prioritize and show love to those at the top first—and then to those at the bottom, if we still had energy at the end of the day. Jesus didn't tell us to have the bleeding victims of greed answer a three-part questionnaire to determine their worthiness before intervening on their behalf. Jesus affirms that neighborly love is merciful love, regardless of the giver or the recipient, and tells us that we are to go and do likewise.

1. Miller, *Animal Ethics and Theology*, 15.

—— 8 ——

The End and the Now

WHEN I SAT DOWN to write this chapter, I had an old song stuck in my head. Maybe you'll know it, about getting to heaven and it being a day of rejoicing and how there will be singing and shouting for victory? Or how about chariots coming for to carry us home? By no means will this chapter be an exhaustive review of eschatology, but I do want to point out some hints we see in the biblical texts that the reconciliation of all things to Christ and worship of him includes nonhuman animals. Jesus's life inaugurated the reign of God, though that reign has not yet been fully realized. In this tension, Jesus followers are called to help foster a world "on earth, as it is in heaven."

Although I grew up in the church, the teachings that I remember about heaven and the kingdom of God and the end of the world were a hot mess that left me confused and skeptical. In humility and with a willingness to learn, I offer the following understanding: Jesus came to announce that the kingdom of heaven was at hand, and he did that over and over throughout the gospels (cf. Matt 4:17; Mark 12:34; Luke 17:21). Of course, if the reign of God were fully realized, we'd be whooping it up in a world with no pain or suffering and *that* obviously isn't the case. Instead, we are living in an age of the "already, but not yet," where Christ "inaugurates living in peace as the present possibility of the future which is yet to come."[1]

In other words, through the risen Christ, relationships that have been marred by sin exist alongside the real possibility of restoration, and we are called to live into that promise *now*, not to fall into the paralyzing mindset that says "this world is not my home, I'm just a passin' through." We may

---

1. Linzey, *Christianity and the Rights of Animals*, 49.

acknowledge that our current earthly existence prevents perfect wholeness, but that is never an excuse to sit idly by and shake our heads sadly at suffering, neglecting to work within and through the restorative power of Christ, fueled by love and the pursuit of holiness. Aware of the suffering and pain experienced by animals raised and killed for food, with a knowledge of the immense waste of natural resources and subsequent impact on both our fellow humans and the rest of creation, and acknowledging that flesh is not a dietary necessity for the vast majority of Western humans, why would we continue to participate in a system that dishonors God's creation and perpetuates violence on a truly phenomenal scale?

For many years, I read the Bible and glossed over the prominent role played by animals, especially in the prophecies and book of Revelation. But a closer look reveals the extent to which God's reign will impact the entire creation. Revelation 4:9–10 envisions "living creatures" giving "glory and honor and thanks" to God, leading the twenty-four elders to do the same. One of those living creatures is like a lion, another like an ox, another like a human, and the last like a flying eagle. The human creature serves the same function in this vision as the other living creatures. That function? To worship God.

Revelation 5:13 foresees "every creature in heaven and on earth and under the earth and in the sea, and all that is in them, singing" in worshipful praise to God. In Revelation 19:4, the elders and the living creatures fall down and worship God. In this world, "he will wipe every tear from their eyes. Death will be no more; mourning and crying and pain will be no more, for the first things have passed away" (Rev 21:4).

The prophetic visions of the Hebrew Scriptures discussed in chapter 4 and these images from Revelation are mirrored throughout the New Testament. The constant theme is that God is the creator of all and that, through Jesus, all the broken and miserable things of the world will be gathered and reconciled to God (cf. John 1:3–4; Eph 1:9–10; Col 1:15–20). Acts 2:17 declares that the Holy Spirit will be poured out on *all flesh*, and Romans 8 recalls Isaiah 11 in its vision of a peaceful, fully reconciled future for all of creation:

> I consider that the sufferings of this present time are not worth comparing with the glory about to be revealed to us. For the creation waits with eager longing for the revealing of the children of God; for the creation was subjected to futility, not of its own will but by the will of the one who subjected it, in hope that the

creation itself will be set free from its bondage to decay and will obtain the freedom of the glory of the children of God. We know that the whole creation has been groaning in labor pains until now; and not only the creation, but we ourselves, who have the first fruits of the Spirit, groan inwardly while we wait for adoption, the redemption of our bodies. (Rom 8:18–23)

While one could (if one were really desperate not to include nonhuman creation in the vision of shalom) argue for a metaphorical reading of the texts or dismiss the significance of the many references to a reconciled creation, Linzey asks, "Can it really be so difficult to grasp that the God who performs the demanding and costly task of redeeming sinful man, will not also be able to restore the involuntary animal creation which groans under the weight of another's burden?"[2] Eating meat and other animal products, ripping animals from their natural habitats and forcing them to perform for us, and raising and killing animals so the rich can wear their skins, among other widespread practices, increases creation's groaning. As disciples of Christ, as bearers of God's image, and as witnesses to the good news, shouldn't we be working to diminish those pangs and reduce suffering?

The biblical texts clearly set out a vision for a world in which God's original peaceful design is restored, a world in which pain and suffering are no longer known, a world marked by nonviolent cooperation within and between species. May it be so.

2. Ibid., 35–36.

$$— 9 —$$

The Bible Tells Me So . . .

So far, I've attempted to articulate a reading of scripture that calls for animal liberation. You may or may not be with me 100 percent, but I hope you are thinking about human-animal relationships in a more complex way than when we began. I hope you are more aware of the ways in which our might has been used for evil means. I hope you are thinking in a new way about what it means to be made in the image of God. Where I've used specific passages to make a point, I hope I've been clear that my interpretation doesn't hinge on a turn of phrase or an obscure fact but on overarching principles and values that many Christians claim to hold, principles and values that have been carried through time by the mothers and fathers of the faith.

I have been having conversations about the Christian faith and animals for more than a decade. Because I take the Bible seriously, I have had to wrestle with some of the passages that my friends and family (and some perfect strangers) brought up in those conversations. Chapter 25 is called "Frequently Asked Questions" and addresses lots of the non-theological questions folks have, but this chapter deals directly with some of the most common verses, counterarguments, and justifications that I've encountered since I began working in animal advocacy. What follows is my best thinking today on these questions. You may disagree with some of my interpretations or conclusions, and I welcome your thoughtful feedback as we embark on this important discussion.

Does it really matter to God if I am vegetarian? Is eating meat or going to the circus or wearing leather sinful?

Sin can be personal or structural, meaning that an individual can commit sin and also that sin can be the result of a social structure specific to a cultural context. Slavery was a structural sin (the institution) as well as an individual one (those who participated in the institution). Persons in the Bible participated in activities and institutions that many mainstream Christians now consider sinful, such as polygamy, stoning women who had sex outside of marriage, and slavery.

At the most basic level, sin is what separates us from God. Sin keeps us broken, fractured, and hurting. Sin is a barrier to shalom, the complete reconciliation of all with God. So, when our use of nonhuman (and human) animals subverts God's creative intention for those sentient beings; when we willingly engage in activities or structures or traditions that cause suffering; when our desires create danger and destruction for others—yes, that is sinful. That said, I have no intention of standing in front of my hamburger-eating friends and screaming "Repent, sinner!"

My life is not without sin. I am a broken being and I seek Christ for healing. And I participate in behaviors that I know are wrong. While ignorance is not an excuse for continued participation in sinful structures, I think we can all afford one another a little grace and guide each other gently toward ways of living and being in the world that bring healing and hope instead of harm. So, when my friends ask me where their chicken breast came from, I am going to be honest and kind, and I hope they will respond to me with the same love when they see opportunities to disciple me.

In a world where millions of people are dying every year from preventable causes and without Christ, shouldn't we focus on more important things? Animals simply aren't a priority of the God we serve.

When my husband and I were dating, he had a friend who lived in a nearby solidly middle-class suburb. Every time we visited, I noticed two dogs in the well-kept yard. They were usually barking—a sign of boredom. One particularly frigid evening, the dogs were outside barking, and I went across the street to ask the family if they planned on bringing the dogs inside. They did not respond well, and my husband's friend was angry that I had said something. He told me that I needed to "pick my battles." Before I was a parent, I didn't pick battles, and when it comes to suffering, I still don't.

All suffering is painful, and it's all connected. We suffer and the world suffers because of that grasping for power that we talked about in chapter 5. Out of generosity and love, God created the whole world—every hair and feather and molecule—and God shared the governance of that world with what God had created. But humans really messed up this beautiful harmony by greedily grasping for more. So now the whole world groans, waiting for reconciliation. And while I am called to make animal advocacy a priority in my life, you, dear reader, do not have to work for PETA full-time in order to make an impact on the nonhuman world. You can minister to the people in your community. You can bring the good news to your company's boardroom. You can stand in solidarity with hungry and oppressed humans throughout the world . . . and simultaneously make choices that decrease animal suffering. It's not an either/or choice. It's a both/and view of the world. I care about both humans and nonhumans, because all brokenness is painful to God.

A biblical concern for animals is not a new concept. The Hebrew Scriptures pretty clearly demand that animals not be treated as inanimate objects. Like humans, animals were to rest on the seventh day (Exod 20:10); oxen are to be unmuzzled, so they can eat while working (Deut 25:4); plowing a field using animals of different species was forbidden, presumably to prevent suffering (Deut 22:10); and the Torah instructs humans to assist an animal in distress, regardless of the circumstances (Exod 23:5; Deut 22:4).

Animals are included alongside humans in the circle of God's concern throughout the remaining Hebrew Scriptures, far beyond the simple call to basic welfare given in Proverbs 12:10. In many cases, nonhuman animals are portrayed as responding to God in worshipful, reverent ways. Psalm 104 is one example of such a portrait:

> O LORD, how manifold are your works! In wisdom you have made them all; the earth is full of your creatures . . . These all *look to you* to give them their food in due season; when you give to them, they gather it up; when you open your hand, they are *filled with good things*. When you hide your face, *they are dismayed*; when you take away their breath, they die and return to their dust. When you *send forth your spirit*, they are created; and you renew the face of the ground. May the glory of the LORD endure forever; may the LORD rejoice in his works . . . (Ps 104:24, 27–31)

These glimpses of the nature of God's spirit in animals are seen again in the third chapter of Ecclesiastes, whose author laments evil, saying,

> I said in my heart with regard to human beings that God is testing them to show that they are but animals. For the fate of humans and the fate of animals is the same; as one dies, so dies the other. They all have the same breath, and humans have no advantage over the animals; for all is vanity. All go to one place; all are from the dust, and all turn to dust again. Who knows whether the human spirit goes upward and the spirit of animals goes downward to the earth? (Eccl 3:18–21)

One possible reading of this text is that humans, in their wickedness, are taking on "beastly" characteristics, becoming "like animals," a very negative view of both and language that mirrors the racist lexicon used to refer to people of color throughout much of United States history. Perhaps the passage points to the vanity of human arrogance concerning their "own" strength and ability, calling instead for the faithful to "stand in awe before him," recognizing that "that which is, already has been; that which is to be, already is; and God seeks out what has gone by" (Eccl 3:14–15). I have a pastor friend who, when questioned about her vegetarian diet, says, "I don't eat my fellow worshippers." The whole earth responds to God, because the whole earth is created through God's spirit.

Didn't God clothe Adam and Eve in animal skins and give every slithering thing on Earth to humans to eat after the flood?

What happens if we read these passages as concessions to the reality of a newly broken world rather than divine permission? And if that is the case, what do we think about these concessions in light of the reign of God incarnate through Jesus Christ?

Because of human greed, the harmony of Eden was destroyed. People suffered and animals suffered. The peace of the earth was shattered and in its place was toil, sweat, and conflict. But you know what the one righteous man in all the earth did before God raised the floodwaters?[1] He followed God's command and saved a bunch of animals. I'm just sayin'. My friend Darren wonders if God kills animals and clothes Adam and Eve because they didn't know how—maybe killing just wasn't in their nature.

---

1. Middleton, *Liberating Image*, 296.

The world is full of evil. But we don't throw up our hands and say, "Oh well, too bad, it's all terrible, so I might as well dive in and be terrible, too!" We roll up our sleeves and figure out how we can love, how we can serve God, how we can foster a world on earth as it is in heaven. We stand with those who are oppressed and marginalized and we stand against powers and principalities that seek to undermine reconciliation and peace. So, yeah, God made clothes of skins for Adam and Eve when he booted them out of the garden. And after the flood, God confirmed to Noah that animals were going to experience fear and dread because of humans. But it doesn't follow that we should go out of our way to *cause* fear and dread. Jesus showed us in myriad ways that we must reject the status quo. So, instead of being complicit in the horror of factory farming, using animals for their skins, ripping them from their natural environment, and so on, shouldn't we do what we can to avoid being the cause of suffering and to attempt in our small ways to restore the harmony of Eden?

Didn't God require animal sacrifices? Doesn't that mean we can eat them?

For a variety of reasons, Christians no longer sacrifice animals to God. The writer of Hebrews 8 and 9 calls Jesus the mediator of a new covenant, which no longer requires the blood of cows and goats. If the question shifts to why God allowed so much bloody animal sacrifice, I have to admit that I do not know, that I am still seeking an answer to this question. I only know that I am under no obligation to kill, either for worship or nourishment, and for that I am grateful.

"It's not what goes into your mouth that defiles you but what comes out." (Summation of Jesus's teaching in Mark 7:14–23)

In this passage, Jesus is challenging the religious leaders for their hypocrisy, for valuing piety above ethics. Jesus wants us to prioritize ethics, the heart-stuff that informs our relationships with God, with each other, and the world. Look at verses 20 and 21: "For it is from within, from the human heart, that evil intentions come: fornication, theft, murder, adultery, avarice . . . all these evil things come from within, and they defile a person." Jesus's teaching recalls the prophetic call for "mercy, not sacrifice," an option afforded to many of us three or four or five times a day, whenever we sit down to eat. When we knowingly consume products that are the result of cruelty and suffering, we are like the religious leaders who value piety above ethics.

"Take, Peter, kill and eat."

This exhortation is found in Acts 10:9–16, but keep reading all the way through to the end of the chapter. While Peter is waiting for some food, he has a hunger-induced dream (v. 10) in which he hears God tell him that what God has called clean, Peter must not call profane. The dream "greatly puzzles" Peter, who doesn't know what to make of it. The next day, at the prompting of the Holy Spirit, Peter goes to the home of a Roman centurion (an astonishingly inclusive act, as a good Jew would never have darkened the door of a Roman soldier). At the house, the Gentiles who are gathered receive the Holy Spirit and are baptized in the name of Jesus Christ. The meaning of Peter's vision is suddenly clear to the reader. Through the vision, God is reminding Peter to remove barriers of fellowship and to reconcile with those from whom we have been separated in order to further the reign of God on earth. In a time when the early church was wrestling with their identity as Jesus followers, this vision is one of radical inclusion. Had Peter followed the religious laws for Jews at the time, he could have never entered a centurion's home and fellowshipped with non-Jews. The borders of the kingdom are porous. In our time, as we wrestle with how best to follow Christ, who are *we* being called to include?

But, yo, Jesus ate fish and stuff, even after the resurrection.

Well, that depends on which account you read. In Luke, Jesus asks for food, is given a piece of broiled fish, and eats it. In John, Jesus cooks fish for his disciples, but isn't explicitly recorded as eating. Jesus may have eaten a little fish in his time on earth—it's pretty likely, given his cultural-historical context—but that simply doesn't justify the systematic way we breed, mutilate, and slaughter tens of billions of animals each year. Even if you think you're living by the letter of the law while eating flesh, is your choice an ethical one? Does it further the kingdom? Does it reconcile or relieve suffering?

In Romans, Paul says don't judge people who eat meat.

Yes, Paul says, "Those who eat must not despise those who abstain, and those who abstain must not pass judgment on those who eat; for God has welcomed them" (Rom 14:3). No doubt. See above re: I'm a sinner and get a lot of things wrong. I hope that if you do start to consider how your actions impact animals you will have grace for those who are not yet ready to do so.

When I was pretty new to animal advocacy and just starting to work out what that meant in terms of my understanding of God, I was talking to some high school students who felt they were being called to the mission field. They were concerned that even if they adopted a vegetarian diet in the U.S., they would soon encounter cultures where to decline the food offered to them would be insulting, would damage the possibility for relationships. I didn't know how to answer them then, but after doing some traveling and praying over the last decade, I think I have some clarity on the subject.

In my experience, I have been able to graciously decline meat in a variety of contexts. In some cases, this has meant transferring a piece of meat that I have been served to the plate of a companion. But more often than not, my abstention doesn't have to be stealthy. At a particularly intimate dinner in Beit Sahour in the West Bank of Palestine, I told the hostess that I was fasting from meat, ate loads of vegetables and rice, and let her know how delicious the food was and how grateful I was for it. There were moments at a home in Nicaragua (where the chicken running over our feet at the breakfast table one morning was on the plate that night) when I wondered if I shouldn't just eat. After all, the chicken had had a lovely life pecking around the property, chasing the pigs, nestled in with her brothers and sisters at night. And she had probably died a fast, relatively painless death. But I looked at the food on my plate—the beans and rice, the hand-made corn tortillas, the avocado and potatoes—and I realized that even if the chicken had had a nice life and a good death, I didn't need her flesh to sustain myself. I had an abundance of plant foods in front of me that would give me fuel for a long day. I needed nothing more.

Paul in Romans wants to let the new church know that we need to be gentle with one another, to build one another up instead of passing judgment on one another. To work on reconciling these broken relationships and structures. In the context of the early church, how Jews and Gentiles were to interact and fellowship with one another was a hugely important question, and which foods were right and wrong to eat was representative of that particular issue. Today, in the United States, we might replace "eat meat" with "vote Republican" or "support gay marriage." I have grown up in an era when the church was *deeply*, dangerously divided on issues. The more entrenched we become in our own views and the less we resolve to listen and be in relationship with those who think differently than we do, the wider the divisions grow. I imagine Paul would weep at the ways in which we've found to vilify one another, while claiming to be Christ's disciples.

And what does that have to do with animals? Everything. Animals are sentient, God-created beings who should be included in our practice of care, our theology of love. But if you're not there yet, I still want you to come over to my house for a delicious vegan dinner.

Intersections and Bridges

(THE OPPRESSION CONNECTION)

Introduction to Part Two

WHEN WE BEGIN TO speak of nonhuman creation, or of caring for God's work, inevitably someone will ask why we are spending time helping whales and owls (or chickens and pigs) instead of other humans, when there are so many pressing problems facing our own species. The morning that I finished the first draft of chapter 3, twenty-six people, including twenty children, were gunned down at an elementary school in Connecticut before the attacker took his own life. That same day, twenty children were also attacked at a school in China, and God only knows how many other children lost or feared for their lives throughout the world. Violence, oppression, and tyranny do not happen in a vacuum; they are systemic, connected, and breed more of the same.

The same misshapen idea of who we humans are as God's creatures and how we are to interact with other creatures, the same brokenness that allows humans to abuse nonhuman animals, also fuels the systematic oppression and abuse of humans by other humans.[1] Aristotle considered it as natural for humans to hunt animals as it was to enslave those for whom slavery was "intended by nature."[2] The same lack of empathy that allowed early vivisectors to justify dissecting live animals in the public square, calling their screams the sound of machines, led the U.S. government to confiscate the bodies of Native Americans after skirmishes and battles in the West, conduct experiments on them, and put them on display.[3] The same mindset that feeds "white racial narcissism"[4] and allows our society to assume bad things are black and good things are white fosters language

---

1. Studies have repeatedly found that violence toward animals in childhood and adolescence is predictive for violent behavior in adulthood. See, for instance, Flynn, "Why Family Professionals Can No Longer Ignore Violence toward Animals."

2. Aristotle, *Politics*, 14.

3. Woodley, *Shalom*, 95.

4. Williams, *Sisters in the Wilderness*, 94.

patterns that devalue nonhuman animals. "Dumb as an ox," "filthy as a pig," and "bird-brained" all perpetuate negative stereotypes of nonhuman animals and set them apart as other.

Our abuse of God's creation comes at a physical price as well. We *must* reverse the pattern of destruction and domination of creation that has marked the last two thousand years of human history, since "nature protests against its rape by modern industrial society through its silent death or through counter-evolutions like Aids [sic], algae and so on. In such a collapse human beings will die out. The earth will survive without them."[5] But in a world filled with pain, it is critical to know it is entirely possible to work simultaneously for the reconciliation of *all* creation to right relationship with one another and with God. One can feed and shelter the homeless person *and* the dog, while working against the systems of oppression that create and sustain poverty. Such an approach is truly holistic.

Catholic theologian Sallie McFague suggests that our first step toward this holistic view of our place in the world, and our responsibilities therein, might be "to look at ourselves from the earth up, rather than from the sky down."[6] When we pause to take this look, to listen to the whole of creation, we are sobered. We begin to hear creation groaning, we become prophets who hear the "silent sigh."[7]

The destructive practices from which the church as Christ's followers ought to divorce itself are too numerous to list here,[8] so we will focus mostly on the issues surrounding the use of animals for food. Jürgen Moltmann points out that "industrial, hormone-controlled 'animal production' is not only brutality towards animals but is also highly detrimental to human health . . . it is also impossible to realize human rights without at the same time noting the rights of plants and the earth."[9] Most Euro-Western Christians are so steeped in the tradition of dominance or in its progressive-but-inadequate cousin, stewardship, that taking even one small step toward reconciliation can be an overwhelming challenge. But step forward

---

5. Moltmann, *Creating a Just Future*, 13.

6. McFague, *Body of God*, 103–4.

7. Heschel, *The Prophets*, 9.

8. Allow me to name just a few: wasteful consumerism that leeches the earth of its limited resources, genetic manipulation and physical mutilation of nonhuman animals raised as human food, subsidizing corporations that clear-cut forests in the Global South in order to graze beef cattle, and ignoring the cries of a billion hungry people.

9. Moltmann, *Creating a Just Future*, 69.

we must, since "Christian understandings of redemption do not concern only hopes for the future, but also entail action in the present."[10]

> Because Christians are made in the image of God, and called by God to a life of relationship and love with all God's creation, Christians should not eat animals . . . [since] loving someone means not eating him/her.[11]

This first small gesture of solidarity, this thrice-daily opportunity to choose nonviolence and reconciliation over violence and separation, can begin the long, slow journey to shalom. When peace begins on our plates, when we intentionally separate ourselves from suffering in the daily ritual of nourishing our bodies, we can begin to consider how to heal other bodies. When we choose to serve and glorify God alongside the rest of God's creation, we more clearly image the incarnated Christ, the One who conquered death to bring new life.

So, here's a quick chapter breakdown of the following section.

Before we spend much time working to prevent animal suffering, we should probably establish that they do suffer, and that it matters. In chapter 10, I'll draw on research from ethologist Marc Bekoff and include a story about spending months researching whether lobsters feel pain when they are boiled or steamed and whether an invention called the Crustastun could help slaughter crustaceans more humanely.

Chapter 11 explores how a deeper understanding of the Trinitarian God can inform our choices and actions related to other created beings. One of the things I think we're good at doing is looking back at the past to see where we were wrong. We've eventually come to realize that forms of oppression which at one time we deemed acceptable are wrong and we've rejected them. I hope that one day we can do that for animals.

Chapter 12 is a brief discussion of what it means to be a human, and an overview of a project that I helped design and implement at PETA that compared historical injustices to modern-day abuses of nonhuman animals.

In chapter 13, we'll look at how the theologies that inform the progressive evangelical's relationship with oppressed and marginalized individuals and sinful structures are readily and necessarily applied to our relationships with animals. I'll make the case that animals are among the most

---

10. Clough, *On Animals*, 170.
11. Largen, "Christian Rationale for Vegetarianism," 151.

marginalized beings today and that human abuse of animals has profound impacts not only on the abused but on the abusers as well.

We'll go a little green in chapter 14 and talk about the inadequacies of creation-care theologies that don't include a radical revision of how humans relate to animals.

In chapter 15, I'll alienate meat-eating lefty peaceniks and point out that using animals necessitates violence. It doesn't take a great leap to get from the theology of pacifism or nonviolence against humans to one that also embraces nonhuman animals. We'll take the leap together.

There are really good arguments for vegan diets based on human health. And probably we can say that this is good and right, since our bodies are temples of the Holy Spirit, etc. But underneath the vegan-as-health mentality is the same vision of human-self as miniature God that got us into this mess in the first place. I think we can have a better theology of embodiment and still save some animals. That's what chapter 16 covers.

No, let's not kill two birds with one stone or beat a dead horse. I am also happy to eat like a pig, thank you very much, and be as dumb as an ox or a birdbrain. Chapter 17 is a short list of alternatives to commonly used sayings that reinforce some negative ideas about the rest of creation. It is placed there as a light-hearted break, not as a diatribe. I hope you read it as such.

Some of the undercover investigations that I saw at PETA will be with me forever. In chapter 18, I'll describe some of the footage and talk about how a group of animal activists, most of them atheists, process suffering and how this impacts their view of God and Jesus followers.

10

Do Animals Suffer?

(AND DOES IT MATTER?)

In a Tibetan village I noticed a crowd of people standing under a burning tree and looking up into the branches. I came near and discovered in the branches a bird [who] was anxiously flying round a nest full of young ones. The mother bird wanted to save her little ones, but she could not. When the fire reached the nest the people waited breathlessly to see what she would do. No one could climb the tree, no one could help her. Now she could easily have saved her own life by flight, but instead of fleeing she sat down on the nest, covering the little ones carefully with her wings. The fire seized her and burnt her to ashes. She showed her love to her little ones by giving her life for them. If then, this little insignificant creature had such love, how much more must our Heavenly Father love His children, the Creator love His creatures![1]

I LOVE THIS STORY from Indian Christian missionary Sadhu Sundar Singh. Singh knew pain and suffering. He was a Saul-like persecutor of Christians at the turn of the twentieth century, a response to the early death of his mother. In deep pain, Singh resolved to kill himself but was instead given a vision of Jesus and became a believer. Singh's remaining family rejected him, but he was embraced by the Christian community and dedicated the rest of his life to service and mission in the name of Christ.

Jesus and Singh both use mother birds to describe God's love.

We humans have a bad habit of saying that anyone who ascribes emotion or intention to nonhuman animals is "anthropomorphizing"[2] them. As

---

1. Singh, *Wisdom of the Sadhu*, 152–53.

2. Anthropomorphizing originally referred to humans ascribing their own

if human animals have a lock on love, fear, pain, or joy. But our experience tells us that is far from the truth, no? Our dogs are gloriously delighted to see us when we return home, no matter how long we've been gone. Canine devotion has been documented from Homer (the Greek, not the Simpson) to legends of canine companions who stand loyally over their human guardian's graves. We've even got an adjective for it: dogged.

Dogs, of course, are a ready example of easily identifiable emotion. They'd make terrible hipsters, their hearts openly displayed on their fur for all to see. But there are countless tales of nonhuman animals who demonstrate emotional and, yes, moral behavior.[3] A dog who tried desperately to rescue a human infant from a burning home; a mother gorilla who, rather than attack a human child who had fallen into her zoo enclosure, picked the child up and gently deposited him near the cage door; the blind doe who was guided through the forest for years by her mate, the fur on their sides worn from constant contact with one another, their arrangement only discovered after the mate was gunned down by a hunter; rhesus monkeys who, forced to administer an electric shock to another rhesus monkey in order to be given food, choose to go hungry instead. Incidentally, when a similar experiment was done in which humans *thought* they were administering shocks to another human at the behest of an authority figure, an astonishing 65 percent of the subjects chose to repeatedly "shock" another human, simply because they were told to do it.

I won't take on the job of convincing you that animals can feel pain, or that they suffer during and after painful experiences. Nonhuman animals have central nervous systems and pain receptors, and they cry out. Even the derided and underappreciated lobster exhibits the classic signs of suffering when he is thrown alive into a pot of boiling water.[4] Zoologists, biologists,

---

characteristics to God. That's right: humans are so narcissistic that we are desperate to find ways to distinguish ourselves from literally every other thing, ever. We are *very* invested in being special. Methinks we are dealing with a little species-wide insecurity.

3. Marc Bekoff, professor emeritus of ecology and evolutionary biology at the University of Colorado, Boulder, has done extensive research and writing on the subjects of animal behavior and cognitive ethology (the study of nonhuman animal minds). Though his work is rooted in scientific method, it is highly accessible to nonscientists, and I strongly recommend picking up a copy of *The Emotional Lives of Animals: A Leading Scientist Explores Animal Joy, Sorrow, and Empathy—and Why They Matter.*

4. Yes, lobsters and crabs feel pain, and they suffer when they are boiled, frozen, steamed, or poorly hacked to death. There are some classic responses to pain, including the shedding of limbs, withdrawal from the pain source, the production of chemicals that mitigate pain, and the presence of receptors for those chemicals, that all indicate the

and ethologists are systematically disproving the age-old assumption that animals are incapable of cognition and moral thought. Donald Griffin, a Harvard zoologist who studied animal consciousness from the 1930s until his death in 2003, points out that "the difference between human consciousness and that of any animal is no doubt enormous, but this difference is probably one of degree rather than kind. Total certainty is not attainable, even when we inquire about the thoughts and feelings of our human companions."[5]

Total certainty is not attainable. At one point, colonial powers weren't sure whether the indigenous humans whose land they stole and whose bodies they dominated were capable of feeling pain. And, sadly, this isn't an old, forgotten problem. Modern research has shown that people of color are less likely to get adequate treatment for their pain, receive fewer pain medicines than light-skinned people in pain, and have a harder time obtaining prescribed medications than light-skinned people. In one study, people (including medical personnel) were shown to assume that light-skinned people felt more pain than darker-skinned people.[6] In other words, there is a gigantic empathy gap from human to human. I'm asking us to do a hard thing: to bridge not only that empathy gap between us and our fellow human creatures, but also the creatures with whom we share less DNA, fewer physical traits, and with whom we can rarely communicate.

The Suffering God

We humans have to ask ourselves whether or not the suffering of our fellow creatures matters. And what role, if any, suffering plays in our relationships to God and to the rest of the created world. Though at least one early church parent—Origen—embraced the theology of a suffering God,[7] the dominant position in the church throughout the centuries, influenced by Platonism,

---

ability for an organism to experience pain. So, I don't know, if you wouldn't boil a kitten to death, I'm not sure you should subject a lobster to that kind of horror, either.

5. Griffin, "Afterword: What Is It Like?," 472.

6. Silverstein, "I Don't Feel Your Pain."

7. God love my boy Origen, who bucked the third-century trend toward Greek thought and claimed, "God has taken our ways upon himself, just as the Son of God bore our sufferings. The Father himself is not impassible" (*Homilia in Ezechiel*, 228.35–230.49.) I'm not fluent in seven languages or an expert on church history, so I've been grateful for McGrath's *The Christian Theology Reader*, which is an excellent source for an overview of theological writings from across space and time.

has been that God is impassible—set apart from suffering, unmovable. But the doctrine of impassibility has increasingly fallen out of favor. Dietrich Bonhoeffer, writing from prison, noted that "God lets himself be pushed out of the world on to the cross . . . The Bible directs [us] to God's powerlessness and suffering; only the suffering God can help."[8]

Can a suffering God still be God? Yes. In his book *The Creative Suffering of God*, Oxford theologian Paul Fiddes shows that ours is "a God who suffers eminently and yet is still God, and a God who suffers universally and yet is still present uniquely and decisively in the sufferings of Christ."[9]

But we don't need theologians to confirm what the scriptures tell us. The earliest chapters of Genesis tell us that God grieves and feels sorrow: "The LORD saw that the wickedness of humankind was great in the earth, and that every inclination of the thoughts of their hearts was only evil continually. And the LORD was sorry that he had made humankind on the earth, and it grieved him to his heart" (Gen 6:5–6). We read of God's anger throughout the Hebrew Scriptures. And we begin to anticipate God's suffering in the world and on the cross: "He was despised and rejected by others; a man of suffering and acquainted with infirmity . . ." (Isa 53:3).

Elie Wiesel recounts the horrific story of watching a young boy slowly die on the gallows in a Nazi concentration camp. One of the prisoners, forced to watch the boy's suffering, asks, "Where is God now?" Wiesel's answer: "Here He is—He is hanging here on this gallows."[10]

Why believe in, much less be encouraged by, a suffering God? Fiddes suggests that we believe in a suffering God because our God is love, who suffered in Christ at the cross. God's bodily torture and death was an act of empathy and solidarity that may help make some sense of human suffering. We also believe in a suffering God because ours is a God who continues to work inside God's created community, a work perfected in the Trinity. In other words, though God is suffering with the boy on the gallows, God is not *only* on the gallows. God moves off of the gallows, through and out of the camp, to suffer with others and to continue to create in and guide us through a broken world.

---

8. Bonhoeffer, *Letters and Papers from Prison*, 360–61.

9. Fiddes, *Creative Suffering of God*, 3. Fiddes' four arguments for the belief in a suffering God are found in the second chapter (pp. 16–45).

10. Wiesel, *Night*, 62.

A New Ethical Framework

To develop an ethical framework that matches our eschatological hope, we need to learn to echo the movement of God, to move from what is to what ought to be, to identify the shortcomings of our is-ness and imagine the freeing possibilities of an ought-ness fraught with love. This isn't just a chapter about the theory of suffering. Theories of suffering and theories of evil are useless without action. "In writing theodicies, individuals detach themselves from the realities of sin and suffering. The purpose of most theodicies is to show why the sufferings which people endure and the sins which they commit do not count against belief in God."[11] We must refuse the urge to detach from suffering, and instead, follow the example of our savior and enter in.

What Is?

When it comes to the suffering of nonhuman animals, what *is* is too legion to thoroughly describe here. For a good overview, take an hour or two and watch *Earthlings*, a documentary that covers an array of the ways in which humans use nonhuman animals. Since it is easy for many humans to recognize and empathize with the suffering of, say, a dog or a cat, I'd like to focus for a few moments on a few nonhuman animals whose ability to feel pain and to suffer are often dismissed out of hand.

Fish

Would you drown a dog? Would you have an ethical problem with someone who did? Even if you decided to kill a dog, I suspect it's not likely that your preferred method would be to drown her. You'd likely take her to a veterinarian or, at worst, dispatch her quickly with a bullet to the brain.[12] Drowning a dog is the equivalent of a bullet gone bad—a slow, painful, and

11. Tilley, *Evils of Theodicy*, 231.

12. Please note, I do not hold these two killing methods on equal footing. A humane euthanasia is a peaceful, controlled way to die and a gift to a suffering animal. Being shot in the head *can* be quick, too, but is more likely to be horrifically cruel, as Kentucky resident Mike Crowe discovered when he taped his local animal control disposing of unwanted dogs by shooting them. The dogs were frequently not killed on the first shot, and were often left to suffer on piles of dead and dying dogs before finally succumbing to their injuries or being shot again. See Gutierrez, "Dog-Pound Killings Caught on Tape."

terrifying experience. Yet when we yank fish out of the water, this is what we force them to endure. We take away their source of oxygen and they suffocate to death. You've seen the Ad Council's asthma commercial where the goldfish flops around to illustrate how horrible it is to not be able to breathe? A bit of an empathy gap there, eh?

In her book *Do Fish Feel Pain?*, biologist Victoria Braithwaite states that "there is as much evidence that fish feel pain and suffer as there is for birds and mammals—and more than there is for human neonates and preterm babies."[13] Even Christians who abstain from other flesh will often justify eating fish flesh and sea animals because of the biblical accounts of Jesus eating fish in first-century Palestine. But let's talk about how fish are farmed and plucked from the sea in our time.

Six billion fish are slaughtered for food each year in the United States. About 40 percent of those fish are factory farmed. Factory fish farms are a lot like factory chicken or pig farms—crowded, filthy, and saturated with drugs and other chemicals to keep animals alive long enough to survive the gross conditions. Salmon, a species of fish who will travel nearly one thousand miles in a single season to spawn, live their entire lives in the space equivalent to a bathtub. Because small fish are in danger of being eaten by larger fish, farms constantly sort fish by dumping them over grates of varying sizes, a distressing and dangerous practice. There are no laws or regulations to protect fish on farms. Reports say as many as 40 percent of fish die on the farm before they are slaughtered.[14]

And how does fish slaughter work? First, farmers stop feeding the fish to reduce the waste that will be produced during shipment. Fish are dumped onto conveyers and then bashed on the head, left to suffocate, packed on ice, or their gills are slit. They are not given the benefit of stunning and are conscious through the entire slow process. Fish are cold-blooded animals and it can take up to fifteen minutes for them to lose consciousness when removed from water or packed on ice.

Fish who are dragged up from the ocean fare no better. While their lives may have been a semblance of the one God intended, their deaths are gruesome and painful. Moreover, commercial fishing is blamed for the endangerment and extinction of countless sea animals—entire species of

---

13. Braithewaite, *Do Fish Feel Pain?*, 153.

14. See http://www.peta.org/issues/animals-used-for-food/factory-farming/fish/aquafarming/.

creatures made by God who have been eradicated from the planet because of human greed.

Commercial fishing trawlers are not the boats of Zebedee and Sons Fishery. They are the size of a football field and can stay on the water for months at a time, storing millions of pounds of fish in on-board freezers. There are a few ways that commercial fishing ships capture fish from the depths:

1. Long-lines: many miles of baited and hooked fishing line are released as the ship moves through the water. Fish on these hooks may be left to struggle and bleed for up to four hours before being reeled in.

2. Purse seines: a common method of capturing tuna. It's a giant netted bag to catch fish.

3. Gill nets: gill nets are giant, vertical mesh nets. Fish swim into them and are trapped by their gills (hence the name) and unable to break free. Fish caught in gill nets may suffocate or bleed to death underwater. Those pulled up from the ocean's depths will suffer decompression, their stomachs exploding out of their mouths. On deck, those fish who have survived will be slit open and left to suffocate or bleed to death.

4. Bottom trawlers: these environmental disasters scrape the ocean floor of *all* life, leaving nothing in their considerable wake. Fish in these nets are crushed together, and decompression forces their eyes out of their sockets, pushes their internal organs out through their mouths, and ruptures their swim bladders.

MICE AND RATS

Mice and rats certainly aren't the only animals used in laboratory experiments, but more than one hundred million of them are used and killed for experiments every year. Their lives and deaths are afforded not even the small dignity of basic welfare protections. Their suffering is unseen. In fact, the Animal Welfare Act, the single federal law that provides any protection for animals used in labs, *specifically excludes* mice, rats, and birds. Not only is their suffering unseen, but they themselves are invisible—in the eye of the law, they do not exist.

As a result, humans have come up with some particularly creative ways to torment mice and rats. They are deliberately infected with cancer and a host of other diseases, used for human genetic research, inflicted with pain (often using electroshocks on their delicate paws) in order to study their responses, intentionally addicted to cocaine and other drugs, mutilated in surgeries, poisoned to death, forced to inhale cigarette smoke and other toxic substances, starved or bred to be morbidly obese, and subjected to a host of other cruelties, despite the well-documented facts that nonanimal models provide far more effective and accurate data and that many of these experiments are redundant to those previously performed. If mice in labs become sick, they are not given veterinary care. If their miserable lives aren't ended by pain, disease, or mutilation, mice are disposed of like garbage. Their heads are cut off with a guillotine or scissors or they are thrown alive into freezers. Since mice and rats aren't living beings in the eyes of the law, experimenters aren't required to provide them even the most basic pain relief, and no experiment, no matter how needless, painful or cruel, is illegal.

Mice and rats are able to communicate with one another and have nervous systems. They can feel pain, they form emotional attachments, and they are highly social and intelligent creatures, as anyone who has kept mice or rats as companions will tell you.[15] Mice and rats have been shown to express empathy and to care for fellows in need. Rats love to be tickled and will laugh with joy. They love to play, but also have systems for establishing boundaries of fairness and trust.[16]

What Ought to Be: Suffering Outside the Gate

Folks who argue for the use and abuse of nonhuman animals for human benefit claim that nonhuman suffering either doesn't exist or doesn't matter. Despite a reputation for being anti-vivisection, C. S. Lewis actually argued that "a great deal of what appears to be animal suffering need not be suffering in any real sense. It may be we who have invented the 'sufferers' by the 'pathetic fallacy' of reading into the beasts a self for which there is no

15. Though one's ability to communicate or level of intelligence should never determine the measure of empathy, mercy, or grace given.

16. See Bekoff, *Emotional Lives of Animals*, 10–12, 56–57, 93, 95, 99, 130, 138, 140, and 144.

real evidence."[17] Lewis thought it best, bizarrely, to err on the side of cold rationality instead of empathy. This strikes me as an odd stance for a Jesus follower to take, particularly in light of Hebrews 13:

> Let mutual love continue. Do not neglect to show hospitality to strangers, for by doing that some have entertained angels without knowing it. . . . We have an altar from which those who officiate in the tent have no right to eat. For the bodies of those animals whose blood is brought into the sanctuary by the high priest as a sacrifice for sin are burned outside the camp. Therefore Jesus also suffered outside the city gate in order to sanctify the people by his own blood. Let us then go to him outside the camp and bear the abuse he endured. For here we have no lasting city, but we are looking for the city that is to come. . . . Do not neglect to do good and to share what you have, for such sacrifices are pleasing to God. (Heb 13:1–2, 11–14, 16)

"Do not neglect to show hospitality to strangers, for by doing that some have entertained angels without knowing it." It sounds like the writer of the epistle knew something about how to handle the uncertainty that Griffin articulated two millennia later: show love. The word translated in the second verse as "hospitality" is the Greek word *philoxenia* or "love of strangers." The writer is telling us not to forget to show love to strangers, including prisoners and those who are being tortured. Showing love to strangers bridges any empathy gap.

In verse 11, we get to a pretty radical idea. An idea even more radical than "love everyone," which is already revolutionary.

There was a lot of hullabaloo in the early church about sacrifices and food regulations.[18] Early Christians weren't sure if they needed to stick with the Jewish food laws or not. They weren't sure how to reconcile their ancient customs, deep tenants of their religious expression, with this new radical concept of loving, fellowshipping with, and showing hospitality to everyone. Sometimes, they'd be offered meat that had been sacrificed to pagan gods. Should they eat that? Politely decline? Lecture their host? Feed the offending substance to the dog while no one was looking? A goodly number of passages in the Epistles deal with this issue. It was a big deal.

---

17. Lewis, *Problem of Pain*, 137.

18. The modern U.S. church likes to call Jesus the "ultimate sacrifice," and we learn early on in Sunday school that the reason we don't sacrifice animals anymore, even though the Bible tells us to, is that Jesus died. But then we go to a church barbeque. It's all very confusing.

In verses 10–13, the writer of Hebrews is alluding to the practice of making a sin offering on the Day of Atonement, detailed in Leviticus 16. The first seven chapters of Leviticus set out in great detail the processes of various sacrifices. Though fat and blood were not to be consumed, much sacrificed flesh could be eaten, provided some other boxes were checked (the flesh is clean, you're clean, etc.). But on the Day of Atonement, the dead animals (minus their blood and fat) were to be brought outside the gate of the camp and burned. Neither the priests nor the people were to consume the flesh.

Jesus changes everything. The night he was betrayed, he called the broken bread and poured wine his body and blood, the new covenant. Isn't it interesting that through Jesus, blood, which was forbidden, becomes celebratory wine? And that the flesh of the Atonement sacrifice, which was burned, becomes nourishing bread? So the writer of Hebrews goes on to say, "Through [Jesus], then, let us continually offer a sacrifice of praise to God, that is, the fruit of the lips that confess his name. Do not neglect to do good and to share what you have, for such sacrifices are pleasing to God" (13:15–16). Take a little time and read Leviticus 1–7. Sacrifices of praise, the sweetness of wine? This is an astonishing contrast to the blood-and-guts slaughter described in the law. And we remind ourselves of this sweetness, this new reality where our hands need no longer be sticky with the dark blood of a terrified beast, by sharing, by doing good, by loving everyone.

So what's this got to do with nonhuman suffering? In the face of uncertainty—in the presence of an "other" who we may not understand, like, or respect, and who may not deserve consideration—we are reminded that our Christ, the one who atones, the one who reconciles us to our Creator and to one another, lived and died on the margins. Christ was mocked, maligned, and misunderstood. He communicated in ways that even his closest friends did not understand. And for the more than two thousand years since Christ's death, we have created centers of power and pushed others to the margins. The church has done this. Christ followers have done this.

Nonhuman animals are on the margins. They communicate with one another and with us in ways we don't always understand. We dismiss the idea that they may feel pain or suffer, *even though* we are told over and over and over again to err on the side of empathy, to love and to care for those with whom we cannot relate.

Moving from Is to Ought

United Kingdom lawyer Simon Buckhaven was on vacation in France one year when his son decided he wanted a lobster for his birthday dinner. Simon entered a local shop, chose a lobster, and was horrified to see the shopkeeper prepare to plunge the crustacean into boiling water. Lobsters who are boiled or steamed to death try desperately to escape—they thrash wildly, lose limbs, and vomit. It takes a terrifying and painful seven to ten minutes for lobsters to finally succumb to the heat. When Simon learned that boiling was the go-to method for lobster slaughter in England and the U.S., he got to work trying to invent a more humane way to end a lobster's life. Two years later, the Crustastun was born. The Crustastun delivers an electric shock to lobsters and crabs, rendering them insensible to pain within a second, and dead after ten seconds.[19]

We can't all invent machines to make death a little more humane for the creatures humans insist on eating. But there's something Simon did that *everyone* can imitate. Simon saw suffering, felt empathy, and worked to make that suffering known. Simon saw, and then he acted. Mice, rats, and birds aren't acknowledged as sentient beings by the one law that protects them in labs; fish, chickens, and turkeys aren't afforded protection under the Humane Methods of Slaughter Act. Nonhuman animals, created by God with abilities, families, feelings, and the ability to feel pain and to suffer, are waiting outside the gate. Will we go to them? Will we respond to their cries?

19. See http://crustastun.com/.

11

The Trinity and Community

BEING IN RIGHT RELATIONSHIP WITH ANIMALS

AS A MIDDLE-CLASS, NORTH American, light-skinned woman (among other attributes), one of the things I have noticed is that my surrounding culture is very good at condemning our ancestors for their wrongs. Through education, introspection, empathy, and sometimes coercion, we come to realize that certain actions and beliefs that were socially acceptable at one time are, in fact, quite evil. Then we point our fingers at those who oppressed or marginalized others, as if we have a lock on enlightened behavior.

Racism, sexism, and a host of other "isms" that were once viewed as rational and ethical are now (mostly) condemned by the mainstream, though they are still practiced in both visible and invisible ways. As we slowly learn to reject routine oppression after routine oppression of "others," we are better able to love as Christ loved. Where once I saw a body to be used for my gain, I now see a brother or sister made in the image of God, one who shares my breath and substance.

For Christians, this radical inclusion of love is steeped in a Trinitarian theology. A deep understanding and complete adoption of the theology of the Trinitarian God can (and must) inform our choices and actions related to other created beings, because when we all get to heaven, it will be a little awkward to worship God next to the chicken we ate for dinner.

Understanding Trinity

When I was a teenager, a youth pastor explained to me that the Trinity was like water, ice, and steam—the same in substance, but different in form.

That seemed perfectly logical to me. My contentment with the "water-ice-steam" analogy is just one way in which I am an heir of Plato's influence (and this is probably just one of the many heretical theologies that I picked up in my Sunday school classes). I was trying to make the math work, to understand how one (God) could be three (the Trinity). But, of course, "the scriptures . . . know only one divine number—the number 'one': one God, one Lord, one Spirit."[1]

In addition to my mathematical confusion, I did not believe that the threefold nature of God had any impact on my work for a more just world. Speculation about the Trinitarian nature of God seemed to have no practical implications for Christian life, aside from my self-invented assignments for each "member" of the Trinity: God was the judgmental one, Jesus the nice one, and the Holy Spirit was like an antidepressant (but no copay!). Imagine my surprise when I read one theologian's assertion that the Trinity is "the most practical of all doctrines"[2] and began to understand that Trinitarian theology is absolutely critical to Christian ethics and praxis.

It all starts with how we understand the words "being" and "person." I assumed that the Trinitarian persons were individual units, but *hypostases,* the word used by the early developers of Christian theology to describe the three beings of the Trinity, are not discrete units. "Person" and "being" in this sense are not finite and limited selves, existing in a vacuum. These beings are interdependent, existing in mutuality. The *hypostases* of the Trinity are "always perfectly in accord . . . inseparably one even while they are three."[3] Consider, for instance, that Jesus is best understood not as an individual, but through his relationships to God, to the church, and to others. "In the beginning was the Word, and the Word was with God, and the Word was God . . . And the Word became flesh and lived among us . . ." (John 1:1, 14).

Humans may *have* relationships with one another, with the created world, and with God, but "God *is* the relations that God has."[4] God is three persons who have no end and no beginning from one another and who dance together in and through and among every part of this created world and beyond. This dance is called *perichoresis,* a Greek word meaning interpenetration or mutual indwelling.

1. Boff, "Trinity as Good News for the Poor," 196.
2. LaCugna, "Practical Trinity," 679.
3. Placher, *Essentials of Christian Theology,* 57.
4. Cunningham, "Doctrine of the Trinity," 85. Emphasis mine.

We get hints of the generative nature of this dance as we continue in the Gospel of John: "In the beginning was the Word, and the Word was with God, and the Word was God. He was in the beginning with God. All things came into being through him. And without him not one thing came into being that has come into being. In him was life, and the life was the light of all people. The light shines in the darkness, and the darkness did not overcome it" (1:1–5). *All things* come into being through the Word, who is and is with God. The first chapter of Genesis also asserts the generative power of God (perhaps the author of John's Gospel had in mind the creation story): "And God said . . . And God said . . . And God said . . ."[5]

Our triune God exists in an eternal, loving interchange in a way that ought to be a model for humans to emulate. In Romans, we read that the Holy Spirit intercedes "with sighs too deep for words" (8:26) on behalf of the groaning creation. Imagine how the world might look if humans related to God's self, to one another, and to the created world in a dance of mutuality. Imagine how the world might look if we fully dwelled in God and in one another. This vision of the Trinitarian dance gives me hope that Christians can lead the world toward a better way of being.

Practicing Trinity

The practical implications for this understanding of Trinity are stunning. This interaction, this dance between God and creation, is not possible outside of relations. In the community of God, we move through the experiences of life together, toward redemption. It is an often-stumbling movement toward living "God's triune life [where] we are able to see such multiplicity and difference as something for which we can rejoice and be thankful, rather than something that needs to be suppressed by our desire for homogeneity and uniformity."[6] The Trinity not only informs how we are to live in community with one another but also points to the acts of redemption and reconciliation in every part of God's creation. One African theologian points out that "if we believe that humans are created in the image of this triune God, these *perichoretic* relationships serve as a powerful model and source for lives that challenge the notions of the isolated individual, enclosed identity and cozy homogeneity."[7] Every redemptive act

5. Cf. Gen 1:3, 6, 9, 11, 14, 20, 24, 26, 28, and 29.

6. Cunningham, "Doctrine of the Trinity," 85.

7. Vosloo, "Identity, Otherness and the Triune God," 87.

is a step into *perichoresis*, into a loving embrace of communion and away from the barren loneliness of self-seeking.

Sometimes, small steps in this process are deeply meaningful. One theologian uses the word "creatures" and not only "humans" to describe those in communion with God,[8] while others search for a metaphor that adequately captures the nonhierarchical nature of the Trinity.[9] When we begin to see ourselves in relation *to* rather than in power *over* those who have been otherized/marginalized/ostracized by church and society, our beliefs will change. Our actions *will* change.

Trinitarian Ethics of a Creaturely Kind

What Is?

There is a way things are and a way things ought to be. Part of our calling as Christ's disciples, perhaps the most important part, is to look at what *is*, see how that lines up with what *ought to be*, and then work toward that better end, always through the church and with the guidance of the Spirit. I am not making a commentary here on personal salvation, only observing that Jesus's call to discipleship had a lot more action than some of his followers have been led to believe. Trinitarian ethics ought to have a profound impact on our daily lives, both public and private.

All creatures, human and animal alike, were created by God, a fact we often forget, I think, or else why would we justify some of the horrific things we do to animals? Take the humble chicken, for instance, a created being whose affection and protection was noted by Jesus.

About nine billion chickens are raised and killed for food each year in the U.S. Most of them are raised in Confined Animal Feeding Operations (CAFOs) or "factory farms." They are hatched in drawers and dumped onto the floor of a giant shed with tens of thousands of their closest friends. As the chickens grow, quarters get tighter and tighter, and the accumulation of feathers, feces, and urine creates toxic air and can become so dangerous that chickens get ammonia burns and workers must wear protective clothing and respirators to safely enter the sheds. To prevent pecking, workers use hot wires or blades to cut the beaks off of baby birds. To accommodate the high demand for breast meat, agricultural companies breed chickens to

8. LaCugna, "Practical Trinity," 680.

9. Cunningham, "Doctrine of the Trinity," 85.

grow enormous upper bodies. Unable to hold this unnatural weight, their legs often cripple beneath them.

Egg-laying hens are crammed into cages about the size of a file cabinet with five or six other birds, giving each bird the equivalent of a standard sheet of paper on which to eat, sleep, groom, defecate, and urinate. The most basic instinct of a bird—stretching her wings—is impossible. Cages are stacked atop one another in massive sheds. To force additional laying cycles, farmers will keep birds in the dark for two weeks and then in the light for two weeks. These warehouses are noisy and toxic, and hens are kept in these conditions for two years before their spent bodies are sent to slaughter. Dead cagemates simply decay next to living birds. Since male chicks are useless to the egg-laying industry, they are tossed alive into grinders or trashcans, where they are left to die.

The first time most chickens feel the sun or breathe fresh air is when they are on the back of a truck, headed to slaughter. To gather chickens for transport to the slaughterhouse, workers walk through the sheds, grabbing fistfuls of birds at a time and flinging them into crates; this frequently breaks the birds' wings and legs. At the slaughterhouse, workers slam birds into shackles at astonishing speeds. The slaughter line runs the birds through an electric stunning bath, which frequently fails to adequately stun the terrified and flapping birds, and then they are run across an automatic blade, which frequently misses the throat, maiming them instead. Every year, millions of birds are still alive when they enter the scalding tank for feather removal, meaning they drown to death in boiling water.

The underlying view of animals as commodities infects the entire animal agriculture industry. The above practices are standard, common, and legal. The entire process, from birth to death, is designed for maximum efficiency; because of this, the God-given needs of animals and their ability to feel pain or fear are not considered. They are treated as inanimate objects, not sentient beings.

Factory farms and agribusinesses like Tyson, Purdue, Hormel, and others thrive because they dramatically alter God's original creative design. Cows, chickens, pigs, and turkeys, all of whom love to forage, are given a processed diet of grain laced with antibiotics. Teeth are either yanked out or cut down, tails and testicles cut off altogether—without the benefit of painkillers. Cow's horns are gouged or burned out of their heads. Standard agricultural practices dishonor God's creative plan and betray our selfish and power-hungry tendency to elevate our own wants and desires at any cost—costs which include not only cruelty to animals but also injury and illness among farm workers and environmental degradation (billions of animals use a lot of water and create a lot of poop).

What Ought to Be?

"Your Kingdom come. Your will be done, on earth as it is in heaven" (Matt 6:10). *On earth, as it is in heaven.* Jesus's life and teachings point us to what ought to be, and the Christian faith has much to offer those of us in whom God has placed a heart for nonhuman creatures. Jürgen Moltmann observes that "the Christian understanding of the world as God's creation is shaped by the revelation of [God's] redemption in the history of Jesus Christ."[10] We see that God is present in God's creation and that the whole earth groans for restoration to God.

The whole earth. Not just the human parts. And not just *for* the human parts. Moltmann again:

> The kingdom of Glory is the indwelling of the triune God in [God's] whole creation. Heaven *and earth* will become God's dwelling, the surroundings that encompass [God], and [God's] milieu. For created beings, this means that—all together, each created being in its own way—they will participate in eternal life and in the eternal bliss of God who is present among them.[11]

Moltmann's assertion that nonhuman creation will enjoy eternal reconciliation with the Creator is firmly rooted in scripture. Recall that Psalm 36:6 declares, "Your righteousness is like the mighty mountains, your judgments are like the great deep; you save humans and animals alike, O LORD." The Hebrew Scriptures are replete with reminders that God created and is the caretaker of the whole creation.[12]

One pervading theme of the New Testament is that God is the creator of all and that, through Jesus, all the broken and miserable things of the world will be gathered and reconciled to God. Acts 2:17 declares that the Holy Spirit will be poured out on *all flesh*, and Romans 8 recalls Isaiah 11 in its vision of a peaceful, fully reconciled future for all of creation.

10. Moltmann, *God in Creation*, 94

11. Ibid., 183–84.

12. Cf. Isa 11:1–10; 43:15–21; 65:17–25; 66:1–3; Hos 4:1–3; Joel 2:22–28; Mic 4:3–8; 6:8.

In Acts 3:19–21, Peter exhorts the early church to remember that the whole world will be restored to God: "Repent, therefore, and turn to God . . . that he may send the Messiah appointed for you, that is, Jesus, who must remain in heaven until the time of universal restoration that God announced long ago through his holy prophets." Paul echoes Peter in Ephesians 1:8–10: "With all wisdom and insight he has made known to us the mystery of his will, according to his good pleasure that he set forth in Christ, as a plan for the fullness of time, to gather up all things in him, things in heaven and things on earth." In Colossians, Paul again reminds the early church that

> He is the image of the invisible God, the firstborn of all creation; for in him all things in heaven and on earth were created. . . . For in him all the fullness of God was pleased to dwell, and through him God was pleased to reconcile to himself all things, whether on earth or in heaven, by making peace through the blood of his cross. (1:15–16, 19–20)

And remember the persistent visions of the promises of restoration of the whole creation in Revelation?

One might argue that humans are so set apart as *imago Dei* that we need only to concern ourselves with others also made in God's image. But Moltmann points out that it is "the whole person, not merely [the person's] soul; the true human community, not only the individual; humanity as it is bound up with nature, not simply human beings in their confrontation with nature—it is these which are the image of God and [God's] glory."[13] To be made in the image of God means to be made in community, to be bound together with the whole created world for the purpose of revealing God, and *that* is the living out of the Trinitarian, perichoretic dance of God.

To love animals and to treat them well does not diminish the gravity or importance of humans as *imago Dei*. In fact, being made in the image of the Trinitarian God *requires* us to expand our hearts and our reach to the most othered of all others and to include them in our fellowship, as that is precisely what God has done and continues to do.[14] That expansion and inclusion is the very *nature* of God.

By urging my brothers and sisters in Christ to live into the hope and promise of the miraculous reality of a triune God, I am not claiming that humans are able to imitate God, or that we can be truly *like* God. Rather,

13. Moltmann, *God in Creation*, 221.

14. Clough, *On Animals*, 24.

"the images, metaphor, and stories of the triune God fund Christian moral imaginations in a way that . . . has transforming potential."[15] Indeed, if we believe that God is the source of all that is, all that was, and all that will be, then our attempts at reciprocity, reconciliation, and restoration—from the most noble to the most feeble—are *only* possible through that triune God.

Moving from Is to Ought

More and more Christians are coming to realize the scope and severity of human mistreatment of our animal neighbors. Archbishop Desmond Tutu writes,

> I have seen firsthand how injustice gets overlooked when the victims are powerless or vulnerable, when they have no one to speak up for them and no means of representing themselves to a higher authority. Animals are in precisely that position. Unless we are mindful of their interests and speak out loudly on their behalf, abuse and cruelty go unchallenged. It is a kind of theological folly to suppose that God has made the entire world just for human beings, or to suppose that God is interested in only one of the millions of species that inhabit God's good earth.[16]

Pastors and other church leaders can follow the archbishop's lead and do their part to provide their congregations with the theological tools to embrace a Trinitarian ethics that includes nonhuman creation in the circle of compassion and care. Doing so urges their congregations outward and might "play a significant role in facilitating the movement of people away from lives of self-interest and toward an earnest devotion to a Christian way of life."[17]

The move from is to ought is not an easy process, but neither is it arduous. It is not accomplished overnight, but neither are we impotent to foster the change we wish to see. But when considering issues of all creaturely relationships, humans are particularly empowered to participate in the prevention of suffering. What I mean is this: it is as easy to choose a veggie burger as it is to choose one made of cow flesh; it is as easy to purchase personal care products that are not tested on animals as it is to choose products that are dripped into the eyes of rabbits; it is as easy to choose a

15. Vosloo, "Identity, Otherness and the Triune God," 83.

16. "Desmond Tutu on Animal Welfare," par. 5.

17. Bullmore, "Four Most Important Passages," 142.

coat made of synthetic fibers as it is to choose one made of feathers yanked from a struggling goose. In the case of preventing cruelty to animals, our yoke truly is easy.

12

What Is a Human?

Thanksgiving Dinner's sad and thankless
Christmas dinner's dark and blue
When you stop and try to see it
From the turkey's point of view.

Sunday dinner isn't sunny
Easter feasts are just bad luck
When you see it from the viewpoint
Of a chicken or a duck.

Oh how I once loved tuna salad
Pork and lobsters, lamb chops too
Till I stopped and looked at dinner
From the dinner's point of view.

—SHEL SILVERSTEIN, "POINT OF VIEW"

I HAVE BEEN A pro-life activist for as long as I can remember. From a rally at the Idaho State Capitol when I was four to tabling for Oregon Right to Life as a junior higher, to defacing a NARAL sticker decorating a filing cabinet in my high school offices . . . I believed that life began at conception, that abortion hurt women and babies, and that it was my job to stand up for those who could not speak for themselves. I also believed that capital punishment was both morally justified and sound public policy, and I ate animals. In other words, my pro-life stance was myopic, limited to only the lives of unborn human babies.

I still hold to my pro-life views, but they are broader now, and I hope I have become someone who evaluates complex issues with more humility than I did when I was fourteen. I don't think that many people are anti-(human)life or pro-abortion (as in, "Oh, don't you just think abortion is so amazing?! Everyone should get one!"). Conversely, it's unfair to label all pro-lifers as "anti-choice" or "anti-woman."

Being Completely Pro-Life

Advocates who argue for limitations or bans on abortion from a religious perspective usually make the following points:

1. It is wrong to take an innocent life.

2. At several points throughout the Bible, it is clear that God sees and knows humans from the womb. It is also clear, from Genesis to Revelation, that children are blessings.

3. The Christian God is a God of love, justice, and mercy. This point is made particularly known in the person of Jesus Christ, who paid special attention to those who were marginalized and vulnerable.

4. Ultimately, life reigns over death. Abortion stops life and is therefore not a part of the eschatological hope of our new life in Christ.

5. Humans are special, set apart. They are made in the image of God. Therefore, all human life is sacred.

Evangelicals who identify as "pro-life" or "anti-abortion" would likely agree with each of these statements as they applied to unborn babies. George Carlin aptly pointed out, however, that this narrow vision of the sanctity of life translates to "if you're pre-born, you're fine; if you're pre-school, you're fucked."[1]

As I discovered the connections between my evangelical faith and my ethical views of animals, I began to see and identify with the term "completely pro-life," but I was (and am) disappointed that the term is still narrowly defined. Each of the five religious arguments above can extend beyond pre-born human babies to encompass both post-born humans and nonhuman animals. Let's look at each one:

---

1. See Carlin, "Pro Life." Note: it's pretty sweary, like most of Carlin's work.

It Is Wrong to Take an Innocent Life

I used to be an avid supporter of the death penalty. To me, as one committed to justice, it seemed fitting that persons who took the lives of other persons should pay with their own. This book isn't about the death penalty, so I won't go into great depth, but I will say that my support for capital punishment began to wane when I heard these words from Gandhi (okay, actually, it was Sir Ben Kingsley in the biopic of Gandhi): "An eye for an eye only makes the whole world blind." Gandhi wasn't a Christian, but he captured a decidedly Jesus-based principle and forced me to reconsider the place of grace, forgiveness, and love both in my own life and in the lives of others. When Jesus was hanging on the cross, he cried out for his murderers' forgiveness. In physical agony, knowing death would come slowly, Jesus could have called for retribution, but he chose mercy. In their book *Kingdom Ethics*, Glen Stassen and David Gushee argue that Jesus consistently avoided furthering the violent or vengeful teachings of the Hebrew Scriptures and, instead, sought to expose and heal the roots of violence.[2] So, with the help of good teachers, I began to see all the ways in which the Bible was teaching me that mercy and justice weren't mutually exclusive pursuits.

And then I began to apply those lessons to what I knew about factory farms. "If you find yourself unable to consistently apply a principle, then perhaps you need to ask yourself honestly whether you actually believe it is true," Catholic theologian Charles Camosy states in *For Love of Animals: Christian Ethics, Consistent Action*.[3] I believe it's wrong to take an innocent life. And yet, humans are breeding billions upon billions of nonhuman animals for the express purpose of killing and eating them. It just doesn't jive. We're not killing cows and chickens and pigs to protect ourselves. And we certainly don't need their flesh to survive. So, we're taking life for our own pleasure. And this is most definitely not what Jesus would do.

At several points throughout the Bible, it is clear that God sees and knows humans from the womb. It is also clear, from Genesis to Revelation, that children are blessings.

The scriptures also contain repeated reminders that God sees and cares for the whole of creation, not only us humans. The whole earth is full of the

2. Stassen and Gushee, *Kingdom Ethics*, 197–99, 216.

3. Camosy, *For Love of Animals*, 127.

glory of God, says Isaiah. God's sanctuary is the earth, the psalmist praises. God reminds Job that the Creator sees the mountain goat give birth and gives the hawk wings to soar. The creation waits and groans, assures Paul. A consistent ethic of life should insist that we acknowledge that, like Job, we humans are "of small account."

The Christian God is a God of love, justice, and mercy. This point is made particularly known in the person of Jesus Christ, who paid special attention to those who were marginalized and vulnerable.

I'll address this concept in greater depth in the next chapter. But for our purposes here, I will say simply that if we believe that, as Jesus followers, we are to orient our lives around the eschatological hope of Christ, then we ought to fervently ask Jesus to help our words and deeds be "characterized by salvation, justice, peace, joy, and God's presence."[4] Watch any video or read any account of a farm, slaughterhouse, laboratory, or other human use of nonhuman animals, and then ask yourself if the actions taken by the people who pay for and perpetuate cruel acts are for or against salvation, justice, peace, joy, and God's presence.

Ultimately, life reigns over death. Abortion stops life and is therefore not a part of the eschatological hope of our new life in Christ.

Do you think there will be slaughterhouses in the new Jerusalem? If not, why not start to make choices now that will reduce the demand for flesh and thus reduce suffering?

Humans are special, set apart. They are made in the image of God. Therefore, all human life is sacred.

Over and over, we have to ask ourselves what it means to be made in the image of God. If it's true that we are set apart, what exactly are we set apart for, and how can we live into that privilege? Even more fundamentally: what is a human? What is a person? This is the argument on which all

4. Stassen and Gushee, *Kingdom Ethics*, 60.

others hinge. Some Christians use their idea of personhood as a defense for the exploitation of other creatures. I see it as an opportunity to exercise compassion, restraint, and, most importantly, humility.

Ron Sider broke the evangelical mold in the early 1970s, when he refused to bend biblical principles to fit a Republican or Democratic agenda. Realizing that Jesus is so much more than secular American politics, Sider sought a third way and has worked for decades to apply Christian teachings to political issues. His method—to first establish biblical norms and then evaluate a political issue—flies in the face of party-line politics, and as a result he's not wildly popular. He is, however, wildly compassionate, insightful, and willing to hold uncomfortable and unpopular views. In his influential *Rich Christians in an Age of Hunger*, Sider advocated for the reduction of our reliance on animal protein, so when I picked up his book, *Completely Pro-Life*, I was hopeful for a bit of wrestling on the issue of the human use of animals, particularly for food. Alas, in the first few pages, he shattered my hopes: "Christians speak of the sanctity of human life to refer to the special status humanity enjoys compared to the rest of creation. Today, however, this special status is under attack. Some secular thinkers denounce as 'speciesism' any claim that persons have a higher status than monkeys or moles."[5] When I began studying with Sider at Palmer Theological Seminary, he graciously tolerated my passion to pursue a line of theological inquiry that revolved around nonhuman animals but held to the insistence that humans are special. As a result of this stance, Sider was open to the idea of pursuing animal welfare reform but stopped short of accepting a biblical mandate for "animal rights."[6]

Defenders of legalized abortion frequently claim that the unborn child in her mother's womb is not a "person." There is the possibility of being a

---

5. Sider, *Completely Pro-Life*, 14.

6. I have been avoiding the term "animal rights" and use it here as it was used in the context of my discussions with Sider. For more on animal rights versus animal welfare, see the glossary. I don't use "animal rights" primarily because I am not convinced that scripture affords "rights" (as we understand them in our present historical context) to anyone. The language of "rights" is loaded with secular political undertones and implications. Rather than demanding rights, I would like to allow the Holy Spirit to transform us so that we treat others with dignity, compassion, and love, no matter how different from us they are. Of course, I'm hoping for this idyllic transformation as a light-skinned person who has led a relatively privileged life. A woman of darker pigment would doubtless view the pursuit of rights from a different perspective. So, "rights" language is something I'm still wrestling with, but I hope and work for the same outcomes as those who embrace the language of human and animal rights.

person, but it is not realized until birth or after since, until then, the fetus needs the mother's body for life. I'm not sure any of us are able to survive, much less thrive, without the help of others, but that is a discussion for another time. Many of the wrong-headed arguments that people make to minimize the suffering of animals (they are nonrational, nonlingual, incapable of moral behavior) could also be said of infants, but we don't have baby farms or roast baby legs for Thanksgiving. And the truth of the matter is that science and experience have shown that animals are rational, lingual, moral, and capable of thriving without human interference in their lives.

Genesis tells us that God created sea creatures, birds, land animals, and creatures we call humans (*adam*). The first creation account in Genesis says that before God formed the creature *adam* from the soil, God said, "Let us make *adam* in our image, according to our likeness . . ."[7] In the second creation story, God breathes life into *adam*'s nostrils and then creates other land, sea, and air animals as companions. The likeness of *adam* to God isn't mentioned.

We don't typically believe that God will look like a human being. We don't confine God to the limited human form. To the early Israelites, God came in a dense cloud and spoke in thunder. Genesis 1 says that *adam* was created *běṣalmēnû* (in our [God's] image) and *kiḏmûṯēnû* (according to our [God's] likeness). *Adam* resembles God, having been made to reflect God's manner, God's relationship and activities. In chapter 3, we read John Wesley's interpretation of this creature *adam*, who was loving, seeing, and obeying. This creature doesn't sound like the scraggly creature who greets me in the mirror each morning, pre-coffee. And it's not—the creatures we call humans today are fallen. The magnificent beings to whom God entrusted the care of the whole of creation and in whose likeness we were created are gone. The beings we call humans now are dim reflections of the creatures in whose nostrils God breathed life and whose body God formed from the dust of the earth.

So why are we still angling for special status? Why are we so eager to climb to the top of a proverbial pile of other creatures, so eager to prove our dominance?

For centuries, scientists have been developing and tweaking the way we classify living things. We have separated one from the other again and again, sometimes based on reproductive patterns, sometimes on appearance, sometimes on genetic markers. It's interesting to me that these

---

7. See chapter 3 for a discussion on dominion as it relates to the *imago Dei*.

biological classifications now rely on language of imperial dominance—kingdom, domain, class, etc.—as a way to silo living beings. The process has evolved and complicated as we learn more about the complex ways in which the created world works. We're still learning. Because we're still learning, I wonder if we might extend more respect and compassion to other creatures. Perhaps we might err on the side of grace and inclusion. About unborn babies, Gushee says, "Personhood is a metaphysical notion beyond the possibility of proof ... I would much rather be wrong in attributing too much personhood to the fetus than in attributing too little. Surely the more pernicious tendency in human history has been to err on the side of too much exclusion from covenant community rather than too much inclusion, with disastrous and cruel results."[8] I, for one, would rather be wrong in attributing too much personhood to sentient beings, no matter their biological classification, since any cursory review of human-animal relations today reveals that the human tendency has been to err on the side of exclusion, with cruel results.

What Is: Species Case Studies

While both primates and elephants face challenges in the wild brought on by human cruelty, this section focuses on animals used in captivity, particularly laboratories and circuses.

Primates

Humans and chimpanzees share a great deal of DNA, with differences varying between 1 and 2 percent.[9] For this reason, they are frequently used in laboratories. This presents a particular moral problem, of course. Since chimpanzees are so genetically similar to human animals, we justify vivisecting them, though history has shown that we repeatedly realize the immorality of experimenting on humans deemed somehow deficient in their historical context (orphans, Native Americans and African Americans, developmentally delayed individuals). I wonder how we'll look back on this period in a century or two and how we'll perceive the actions and systems that we take for granted now.

8. Stassen and Gushee, *Kingdom Ethics*, 222–23.

9. See, e.g., Smithsonian Institution, "What Does It Mean to Be Human?"

There are more than one hundred thousand primates currently used in U.S. labs, and about one thousand of those are chimpanzees. Primates are either ripped from their mothers in the wild or bred in captivity. Life in a laboratory is utter misery. While primates in the forest and jungle enjoy miles of trees, grasses, and the company of large extended families, primates in laboratories are individually confined to small steel-and-concrete cages; there is no legal requirement for these cages to be any larger than five feet square and seven feet tall. Experimental drugs are pumped into their stomachs for pharmaceutical tests; primates are intentionally infected with diseases and then used to test new vaccines; they are used for chemical weapons testing and research by the U.S. military; baby monkeys are deprived of all real or simulated maternal contact to study the psychological impacts (newsflash: not having a mom sucks); and they are used in invasive brain experiments where bolts and wires are inserted into their skulls so that vivisectors can record brain activity and cognitive functions.

The pain, confinement, and loneliness cause primates in laboratories to go crazy. They spin or rock endlessly in their tiny cages. They tear out their hair or bite their own arms and legs. They become anxious, depressed, and aggressive. Some primates live for decades in this hell. The Jane Goodall Institute shares the story of one chimpanzee, Karen, who was ripped from her home in the wild as an infant and kept for more than fifty years in a steel box at a Louisiana laboratory.[10] Chimpanzees have been shown to be altruistic, empathetic, playful, inventive, and self-aware. We respond to these God-given qualities by caging and mutilating their bodies and depriving their minds.

Marc Bekoff dedicates one of his books to Pablo, a chimpanzee used by New York University. Pablo was "darted 220 times . . . subjected to 28 liver, two bone marrow, and two lymph node biopsies . . . In 1993 he was injected with 10,000 times the lethal dose of HIV . . . [he died] of an infection aggravated by years of darts, needles, and biopsies."[11] An undercover investigator at the Oregon Regional Primate Research Center observed adult male monkeys enduring "electro-ejaculation," a procedure in which metal bands were wrapped around a monkey's penis and an electrical charge applied to induce ejaculation. One monkey underwent this painful experience more than two hundred times in a nine-year period. Another vivisector at the lab receives

---

10. See Jane Goodall Institute, "Chimps in Captivity," and Humane Society, "Undercover Investigation."

11. Bekoff, *Emotional Lives of Animals*, 27.

$750,000 in government funding each year (your tax dollars at work) to feed pregnant monkeys unhealthy diets and frighten their babies with children's toys.[12] A whistleblower at a facility in Washington State that uses tens of thousands of animals a year to test products for other companies and government agencies exposed the profound physical and psychological violence endured by the monkeys there, including being strapped into restraint chairs for hours at a time while being repeatedly injected with intravenous drugs. Vivisectors at Columbia University gouged the eyes out of baboons and clamped off the arteries to their brains to induce stroke. Many baboons were conscious during these procedures, and none had painkillers.

Elephants

In the wild, elephants stay in close-knit family packs. Female babies will stay with their mothers for decades, and males will separate from their families only as adults. Elephants unite as a group—they gather around sick members and help birthing mothers through labor and delivery. They walk a hundred miles a day, mourn when one of their pack dies, and can recognize the bones of a fallen friend even after many months.

Shortly after I gave birth to my son, I saw a video of a mother elephant giving birth at a Ringling Brothers breeding barn. One front leg and one back leg were tied down; the only movement she was allowed was to rock back and forth. When the pain of labor intensified and she became distressed, she bent forward to rock onto her head . . . a "trick" she had learned through intimidation and beatings and something elephants do not do in the wild. Elephants in the wild are guided through labor by more mature elephant mothers. This young elephant, just a child herself at seven years old, was accompanied through labor by three human handlers, at least one of whom used a bullhook (a heavy rod with a pointed and hooked metal end) to poke and prod the laboring mother into submission. The moment her baby dropped to the concrete floor, handlers rushed in to take him to an adjacent stall. The new mother strained against the ropes and stretched her trunk out to touch her baby, but he was far out of reach.

A few years after that baby was born, if he survived, he was probably taken from his mother to begin "training" to "perform" in one of Ringling's traveling shows. We only know what these training sessions are like because of photographs taken by a whistleblower and released to PETA

12. No, for real, you pay for this. See PETA, "Vivisector of the Month."

after his death. Curious and energetic baby elephants, just three or four years old, are tied down in concrete barns for up to twenty-three hours a day. Every natural instinct is crushed. They are tied down and forced into unnatural poses. They are screamed at and slapped. They are poked and hit with a bullhook, which will be their constant companion for the rest of their miserable lives. Undercover footage of juvenile and adult elephant training and handling shows circus employees using bullhooks to jab elephants in the most sensitive spots of their bodies: under their trunk, behind their ears and knees, around their jaw. They sink the sharp bullhook into the elephant's skin and yank, or they simply swing the bullhook as hard as they can and beat the elephant into submission. New trainers are told to "make 'em scream."

After their spirits have been broken and they've learned the tricks of the trade, elephants are chained in train cars and carted around the country for night after night of circus shows featuring blaring music, screaming children, and more beatings. Elephants may spend up to one hundred hours chained in a boxcar during travel. Every natural instinct is stymied; their lives are long, boring, and painful.[13]

It's no wonder that elephants rampage.

If you're my age, you might remember Tyke, the African-born elephant who was taken from her family and used in circuses. When she was nineteen years old, she escaped her handlers and got loose in the streets of Honolulu. Law enforcement officers shot her eighty-six times. It took her two excruciating hours to finally succumb to her wounds.

What Ought to Be: Living Into the *imago Dei*

When I think about being made in the image of God, I don't think that gives me the right to force a monkey to ejaculate using electroshocks, or to beat baby elephants into submission so my company can make money. And if that's what it does mean, then I want out of the club. There is nothing in Genesis that indicates that being made in the image of God gives humans license to kill. The very opposite is true. We are made in God's image and commanded to *care for* the rest of creation. It's a pretty twisted view of the nature of God if we take our being made in the likeness of God to mean we can mutilate, abuse, torture, and otherwise wreak havoc on

13. You can watch some elephants rescued from bad situations here: https://www. elephants.com/.

God's other created beings. We have struggles, but that isn't how God deals with us human animals. God is so invested in being in communion with the created world that God took on flesh in the form of Jesus, spent three decades showing us how to include outcasts in our daily lives, and bore the weight of the world's failure to do that on the cross. For Christians, animal liberation doesn't come from human action. Animal liberation, like our own liberation from sin, comes from Jesus's victory over death on the cross.

Moving from Is to Ought: Examining Intersecting Oppressions

One of the projects I worked on at PETA was a traveling display called "The Animal Liberation Project." Once you know a little bit about how humans use animals, it's easy to see parallels between what we do to animals now and how dominant human groups have oppressed, marginalized, and otherized groups of humans in our past. Suffragettes on hunger strike were force-fed in prison, tubes forced down their throats; humans hold geese down and thrust metal pipes full of corn mash down their long necks so that we can kill them for their diseased, fatty livers. Enslaved humans were branded, the same way we brand cows today. Brown-skinned men are tortured and imprisoned indefinitely in Guantanamo Bay, just as we imprison primates for decades in labs. Native Americans were ripped from their homelands and herded into tiny reservations, the way we rip animals from their homes and put them on display for our "entertainment." Photographs of row on row on row of starved Jewish prisoners in concentration camps looks a lot like row on row on row of starved hens in egg factory farms.

This project was not wildly popular.

When the display was taken to campuses, it was vandalized. PETA was reviled in the press as racist and anti-Semitic. I wasn't on the road with the display, and after all the negative press, I was surprised that when I went to visit it at the National Mall, the people who actually stopped to look at the images and read the comparisons were largely supportive. It clicked.

I struggle with making these comparisons. As a light-skinned woman of global privilege (though I earn less than about 94 percent of tax filers in the United States[14]), I acknowledge that I do not know what it is like to live with the legacy of slavery or the Holocaust or genocide, and I do not know enough about my ancestors to know if they were active participants in the

14. IRS, "SOI Tax Stats."

oppression of other humans. I worry that I am too far removed from deep suffering to be able to make these suggested parallels authentically.

But I don't make these comparisons to diminish the significance of the suffering endured by otherized humans. I believe that the more we understand about the interconnection and intersections of oppression, the stronger our resolve and the better equipped we will be able to join *all* movements toward liberation made possible by the death and resurrection of Christ. So, I join with Camosy to charge the church: "Not only is commitment to other human causes like racial equality and the pro-life movement not a reason to avoid the animal liberation movement, it is a reason to join it. The Church must and should lead on this new issue of liberation. It is what we do."[15]

15. Camosy, *For Love of Animals*, 132.

13

The Heresy of Hierarchy

BEFORE I WAS A parent, when I had only two jobs, one of them was at a Saturday program for kids in an underserved neighborhood in Norfolk, Virginia. Park Place Child Life Center offered homework support and arts classes during the week, and on Saturdays we provided daylong programing, including karate and dance classes, art, music, theater, field trips, and special events. As a person who generally doesn't like other people's kids, this job was a stretch for me, and there were some kids who were just plain hard to love.

James was among them: he usually showed up late, filthy, and wild. He didn't speak but communicated through grunts and, sometimes, screams. He was never still, never cooperative, never attentive. Though he was just seven or eight years old, I never saw him with an adult. He ran the streets of Park Place alone or with friends. He would frequently become enraged and started to flail at anyone who came near him. Many volunteers and I tried to connect with him, but we very rarely succeeded. His too slim body vibrated with anger, pain, confusion, and chaos. To us, he seemed feral, and he broke my heart and frightened me all at the same time.

One sunny summer afternoon, we gathered the kids in the field of the elementary school across the street from the Baptist church where we held our Saturday program to hear a representative from a local animal shelter. She talked to the kids about caring for companion animals, about what the shelter did to help animals in need and what to do if they came across a stray. Very few of the kids in our group had had positive experiences with dogs and cats. The neighborhood was rife with chained pit bulls. One family had watched as their beloved dog was shot to death by a neighbor, the victim of a petty feud.

It struck me that our kids could identify with the homeless animals the worker brought that day—their lives filled with uncertainty, bounced from place to place, frequently abused, neglected, or screamed at by hurting, frightened, or angry adults. Some of our kids had experienced extreme abuse. Some of the girls and boys took the opportunity at the end of the lesson to touch the animals, others quickly lost interest and left as soon as they had permission to run in the field.

I don't know how long it was before I noticed James. He was crouched next to the fluffy white Husky mix brought by the shelter, absolutely still except for the long strokes his hand made over the dog's head and back. The big dog was equally still, head resting on his paws, relaxing in the sun, enjoying his massage. Their bodies together were soft. A calm emanated from the sacred space that they had entered, as if the world had gone still around them. They sat there together on the grass for what seemed like an eternity, until it was time for the shelter animals to leave and they parted ways.

Whenever I think of the weak and vulnerable, I think of the bond shared by James and the shelter dog. I think of how these two creatures, neglected by the rest of the world, found connection with one another. Because we know Jesus is with those whom society rejects, we know Jesus was with James that day, perhaps talking to him as he stroked the dog's back, enveloping him in the sun and breeze and warmth of gentle love. But I think Jesus was also with the dog, whispering in his ear that this little boy needed to be near a calm spirit and assuring him that though he had been dumped at a crowded shelter and forgotten by much of the world, he was still seen.

The Special Status of the Weak and Vulnerable

Over and over, throughout the entire body of scripture, we see that God cares, and commands us to care, for the weak and vulnerable members of society, including nonhuman animals, widows, orphans, children, the poor, immigrants, and outcasts. We can't possibly cover *all* of the biblical examples in this short chapter, so here is just a taste:

> When you come upon your enemy's ox or donkey going astray, you shall bring it back. When you see the donkey of one who hates you lying under its burden and you would hold back from setting it free, you must help to set it free. You shall not pervert the justice due to your poor in their lawsuits . . . You shall not oppress a resident alien; you know the heart of an alien, for you were aliens

in the land of Egypt. For six years you shall sow your land and gather its yield; but the seventh year you shall let it rest and lie fallow, so that the poor of your people may eat.... You shall do the same with your vineyard, and with your olive orchard. For six days you shall do your work, but on the seventh day you shall rest, so that your ox and your donkey may have relief, and your homeborn slave and the resident alien may be refreshed. (Exod 23:4–6, 9–12)

You shall rise before the aged, and defer to the old; and you shall fear your God: I am the LORD. When an alien resides with you in your land, you shall not oppress the alien. The alien who resides with you shall be to you as the citizen among you; you shall love the alien as yourself, for you were aliens in the land of Egypt: I am the LORD your God. (Lev 19:32–34)

Who is like the LORD our God, who is seated on high, who looks far down on the heavens and the earth? He raises the poor from the dust, and lifts the needy from the ash heap, to make them sit with princes, with the princes of his people. He gives the barren woman a home, making her the joyous mother of children. Praise the LORD! (Ps 113:5–9)

Early on in the Bible, God lays the groundwork for an inclusive compassion. Creating land, air, and sea out of a formless void, inhabiting this new earth with beings so very different from the Creator, then caring for and redeeming it are all acts of inclusivity. And God communicates the necessity of that inclusivity through the laws given to the Israelites. The most vulnerable and marginalized among them—children, widows, the poor, enslaved persons (slavery and poverty being intimately connected), immigrants, and animals—were all singled out for protection against exploitation, overwork, and suffering. These commands are echoed again by Jesus and the early church.

Jesus had just then cured many people of diseases, plagues, and evil spirits, and had given sight to many who were blind. And he answered them, "Go and tell John what you have seen and heard: the blind receive their sight, the lame walk, the lepers are cleansed, the deaf hear, the dead are raised, the poor have good news brought to them. And blessed is anyone who takes no offense at me." (Luke 7:21–23)

If any think they are religious, and do not bridle their tongues but deceive their hearts, their religion is worthless. Religion that is pure and undefiled before God, the Father, is this: to care for orphans and widows in their distress, and to keep oneself un-stained by the world. (Jas 1:26–27)

Jesus's life is a love letter to the oppressed and marginalized (including Roman soldiers, prostitutes, lepers, children, and the poor), and the Gospel of Luke particularly focuses on this aspect of Jesus's ministry. Peruvian evangelical theologian Darío López Rodriguez explores this theme in his short but powerful book *The Liberating Mission of Jesus: The Message of the Gospel of Luke*. Rodriguez points out that from Jesus's first breath, taken in a manger, he is identified "with all the destitute and defenseless of the world."[1] Let's look at just a few examples from Luke:

As the sun was setting, all those who had any who were sick with various kinds of diseases brought them to him; and he laid hands on each of them and cured them. (4:40)

Once, when he was in one of the cities, there was a man covered with leprosy. When he saw Jesus, he bowed with his face to the ground and begged him, "Lord, if you choose, you can make me clean." Then Jesus stretched out his hand, touched him, and said, "I do choose. Be made clean." (5:12–13)

After this he went out and saw a tax collector named Levi, sitting at the tax booth; and he said to him, "Follow me." And he got up, left everything, and followed him. Then Levi gave a great banquet for him in his house; and there was a large crowd of tax collectors and others sitting at the table with them. The Pharisees and their scribes were complaining to his disciples, saying, "Why do you eat and drink with tax collectors and sinners?" Jesus answered, "Those who are well have no need of a physician, but those who are sick; I have come to call not the righteous but sinners to repen-tance." (5:27–32)

Then he looked up at his disciples and said: "Blessed are you who are poor, for yours is the kingdom of God. Blessed are you who are hungry now, for you will be filled. Blessed are you who weep now, for you will laugh." (6:20–21)

"If you love those who love you, what credit is that to you? For even sinners love those who love them. . . . But love your enemies, do good, and lend, expecting nothing in return. Your reward will be great, and you will be children of the Most High; for he is kind

---

1. Rodriguez, *Liberating Mission of Jesus*, 9.

to the ungrateful and the wicked. Be merciful, just as your Father is merciful." (6:32, 35–36)

In Luke, we also learn that eternal life is inherited by those who love God and love their neighbor, and that a neighbor is the one who shows others mercy (10:25–37). We learn that those who live by the law but neglect justice and love are doing it all wrong (11:42). We learn that though sparrows are small and used as throwaway objects by men, God sees and values each one (12:6–7), and that God provides food for ravens (12:24) and clothes the grasses of the field (12:27–28). Of course, Luke isn't the only gospel in which Jesus's inclusion of the marginalized is evident. Jesus's genealogy in Matthew includes prostitutes and Gentiles, and Jesus gives revolutionary instructions for nonviolent action and reconciliation throughout the Sermon on the Mount. Rodriguez claims that "the proclamation of the gospel of the kingdom of God crosses frontiers of every kind."[2]

But while Rodriguez argues for the universality of Jesus's mission, he limits the recipients of this liberation to human beings: "Who are the recipients of the good news of salvation? In a full sense, according to Luke, all human beings are."[3] While I'm not arguing that animal lives need "saving" in the same sense that Jesus saved humans from sin, it does seem clear from scripture that animals, as part of the whole creation, will be included in the reconciliation brought by the kingdom of God. The earth and all of its inhabitants will be healed of brokenness and pain.

It's easy enough to identify the marginalized and oppressed individuals of first-century Palestine from the safe distance of two thousands years. Rodriguez rightly points out that "in order to know the world of the marginalized of our time, we must first come out of the tunnel of indifference, leaving aside *all* of the prejudices that limit the establishment of more inclusive social relations."[4] But in the next breath, Rodriguez sets a limit on that inclusivity. Here are his words, modified by me to demonstrate the ease with which we can extend our vision:

> ~~Human~~ beings are not anonymous bodies without specific identities or life histories, objects that can be manipulated, disposable pieces subject to the invisible hand of the market, figures to nourish cold statistical charts of institutions of the State or of organizations tied to international cooperation. . . . Jesus had come to give good

2. Ibid., 25.

3. Ibid., 38.

4. Ibid., 49, emphasis mine.

news to the poor and the marginalized, to preach the year of the Lord's favor. . . . The same attitude and practices should characterize the individual and collective testimony of the disciples of Jesus. . . . They also must see, not things or statistics, but ~~human~~ beings who find themselves in real situations of oppression. All disciples involved in pastoral tasks, in service projects, and in social action, and connected to the world of the poor and marginalized, must understand that they work with ~~human~~ beings of flesh and bone and not with disposable things.[5]

If today's followers of Jesus obey our calling to cross borders, to go into the uncomfortable places, to identify and stand in solidarity with those whom society has utterly rejected, shouldn't we allow our gaze to cross the species barrier, particularly when the evidence is so strong that they feel pain and suffering?

The Connection between Human and Animal Abuse

When I think about the most vulnerable in our society, of course I think of animals, but I also think of the individual humans, like James, who live in fear and chaos as the result of physical, sexual, or psychological abuse. The "might makes right" mentality that allows one to justify exploitation of the other is the heresy of hierarchy. Heresy is a belief or practice that is wildly variant from the dominant or accepted belief or doctrine of a body. The body of Christ, the church, claims that God is love, that Jesus is the Prince of Peace, the Healer. The body of Christ claims that we must die to ourselves in order to live in Christ, that the merciful are blessed, and that the weak will be made strong. Christ's body was broken so that we could be released from the shackles of sin, of cruelty, of dominating violence. And yet the body of Christ has perpetuated or supported theologies and policies that allow some to come "in" and keep others very far "out." The church, and particularly the American evangelical church, has become very good at training gatekeepers.[6]

We have created a structure, a stairway to heaven, and we know everyone's place on it. But Jesus told us to "do to others as you would have them

5. Ibid., 49–50.

6. Fred Clark, former Evangelicals for Social Action employee, talks a lot about evangelical gatekeeping on his Patheos blog, *Slacktivist* (http://www.patheos.com/blogs/slacktivist/). I've never met Fred, but I get the feeling that he's a bit of a curmudgeon, so I think we'd get along just fine.

do to you." We take it for granted now, but the word "others" in Greek there is kind of radical. It's an encompassing word, meaning all people, everyone. Not just Jews or Gentiles, not just a certain economic class, not a certain gender, but everyone. For Jesus to tell his followers that they should treat *everyone* as they wanted to be treated was revolutionary. It's part of the reason he was killed.

Abusing the weak is cyclical, a self-perpetuating cycle. A study sponsored by the National Institute for Justice found that a child who is abused or neglected is nearly 30 percent more likely to engage in criminal or delinquent behavior as an adult.[7] As young adults, victims of childhood abuse are more likely to be violent toward intimate partners.[8] Further, a host of antisocial behaviors, including interpersonal and intimate partner violence, has been linked to persons who abuse animals.[9] It makes sense on a practical level—think of my concern about James and the shelter dog. James was used to being the weak one, the one who was neglected and abused. Given the chance, it's easy to see how one who was always on the receiving end of evil might choose to return that evil to a weaker, more vulnerable being. But Jesus redeems all.

One's child choosing to be gentle instead of rough may seem like a small thing. Choosing a veggie burger over one made of beef may seem like a small thing, choosing to spend a few dollars on one shampoo instead of another may seem like a small thing, but each of these "small things" cracks the walls that separate the powerful from the weak, the haves from the have-nots, the one from the other, and creates room for redemption, restoration, and love.

Throughout his ministry, Jesus created these cracks. He raised people from the dead and healed horrible illnesses, but he did small things, too. He straightened a withered hand, pointed out the faith of a generous widow, had short but meaningful conversations with outcasts and went over to their houses for dinner. He provided wine for a wedding and food for hungry followers. He had patience with his disciple's thickheadedness and chastised them for trying to shoo children away from him. He let a sinner wash his feet and told stories that helped everyday folks make more compassionate decisions.

---

7. Widom and Maxfield, "Update on the 'Cycle of Violence,'" 3.

8. Fang and Corso, "Child Maltreatment," 281.

9. See, for example, Arluke et al., "The Relationship of Animal Abuse"; Tallichet and Hensley, "Exploring the Link"; and Becker and French, "Making the Links."

Instead of perpetuating tensions, biases, and fears, Jesus gathered rejects together to love them, and so that they could repent and also love. Stopping the cycles of abuse and violence, joining and being welcomed into a radically inclusive Trinitarian life, means that those who are converted to God are also converted to one another, regardless of their previous labels, sins, and sufferings. I wonder how we change when we welcome animals to the table as guests rather than as dinner. I wonder if we begin to see those who are weak and vulnerable as beloveds of God, how we might respond differently to them. I wonder how these small acts of kindness, compassion, love, and redemption might begin to change not only us but also the whole world.

— 14 —

Stewardship of Creation

(OR, CHANGING LIGHT BULBS ISN'T ENOUGH)

And he said to them, "Go into all the world and proclaim
the good news to the whole creation." Mark 16:15

THE YEAR BEFORE I started seminary, the church I belonged to asked me
to put together a creation care program for the congregation. It took a
great deal of continued restraint to not submit a proposal and program
consisting entirely of the words "Go Vegan—You Can't Be a Meat-Eating
Environmentalist" and "Stop Serving Meat at Church Functions." I was the
gal who boycotted the church picnic the year they held it at the zoo, griped
about petting zoos on Easter, begged for veggie burgers and veggie dogs
at every cookout, and raised unholy Cain when I found glue traps in the
building. As the church's only PETA-phile and resident animal activist, I
was worried that the powers that be wouldn't take my advice seriously, that
they would attribute my arguments to sentimentality instead of science.

Many of the Christians I talk to about vegetarianism and animal issues
suggest that I couch the arguments in favor of animal liberation in terms of
green theology, creation care, environmental stewardship, simple living, or
conservation of resources. All valid points, so I have set aside this chapter
to talk about the environmental impacts of our exploitation of nonhuman
animals, particularly for food. What I want to say first is this: if you are
committed to mitigating climate change and practicing environmental
stewardship out of a concern for your own well-being, you are getting it
wrong. The point of caring for the earth is not to ensure preservation of
the human species, it is to be obedient to God's commands and a faithful
witness to the promise of reconciliation through Jesus's resurrection.

Green Theology

Most ecotheologies rightly start with a review of the facts about climate change, perhaps in part to convince the few remaining climate change deniers that we are dealing with a real and serious problem. I am not going to do that here. There are loads of good resources easily available, though I am particularly fond of Young Evangelicals for Climate Action (YECA), which has a website stocked with resources and research.[1] After establishing the frightening realities we now face, green theologies discuss the biblical foundations for creation care, arguing that working to stem climate change does as much good for the earth's inhabitants as it does for the earth.

As you might expect, Genesis is a good place for Christian ecotheologies to start.[2] When God creates humankind, it is in God's image and to "have dominion." God's first words to the human creatures are these: "Be fruitful and multiply, and fill the earth and subdue it . . ." We spoke extensively about the concept of dominion in chapter 3 and about how misinterpretations of dominion to mean "dominate" instead of "steward" have led to the destruction and decay of God's creation. So in this chapter, we will look more closely at that troublesome word "subdue."

There is really no nice way around the word "subdue" (כָּבַשׁ *kabash*). It even sounds violent. And it is. It means to dominate, to tread on, to subjugate. In the Bible, it's used only in the Hebrew Scriptures, and mostly to refer to military conquests.[3] The same word is also used to describe the selling of children into slavery and the rape of women and girls.[4]

But then something really interesting and significant happens. Look at how the word is used in Micah: "Who is a God like you, pardoning iniquity and passing over the transgression of the remnant of your possession? He does not retain his anger forever, because he delights in showing clemency. He will again have compassion *on us; he will tread* our iniquities under foot. You will cast out all our sins into the depths of the sea" (7:18–19). And again in Zechariah 9:

---

1. See www.yecaction.org.

2. I admit, I scoffed a little when I heard that there was a "Green Bible." But it's actually a really helpful resource for those who are interested in exploring the intersection of biblical study and creation care. HarperCollins publishes it. Your local Christian bookstore probably carries it.

3. Cf. Num 32:22, 29; Josh 18:1; 2 Sam 8:11; 1 Chr 22:18; 2 Chr 28:10.

4. Cf. Neh 5:5; Esth 7:8; Jer 34:11, 16.

Rejoice greatly, O daughter Zion! Shout aloud, O daughter Jerusalem! Lo, your king comes to you; triumphant and victorious is he, humble and riding on a donkey, on a colt, the foal of a donkey. He will cut off the chariot from Ephraim and the war horse from Jerusalem; and the battle bow shall be cut off, and he shall command peace to the nations; his dominion shall be from sea to sea, and from the River to the ends of the earth. . . . The Lord of hosts will protect them, and they shall devour and *tread down* the slingers . . . (9:9–11, 15)

The prophets are *reclaiming this word for God's use.* In these passages, *kabash* does not refer to the perpetuation of suffering but to God's victory over that suffering. If we reread the Genesis command to fill the earth and subdue it in light of this proclamation, we can take the charge to subdue the earth as one in which we are called not to wreak havoc but to grant mercy; not to dominate the earth but to quell those forces and systems that might threaten God's peaceful creation.

There are several well-known passages elsewhere in the Hebrew Scriptures that theologians cite in support of an ethic of creation care, including the command for everyone to take a break on the Sabbath (because this gives the earth and all of its creatures a chance to rest); the command to let the earth lie fallow every seventh and fiftieth year; and laws and decrees that made clear that the earth belonged to the Lord, and human creatures were its tenants.

This respect for the land continues into the New Testament. Native American theologian Randy Woodley points out that as a carpenter, Jesus could have used mechanical metaphors to illustrate his points; he could have told stories about building, about wheels and angles and geometry. Instead, Jesus told stories rooted in the land, in agriculture, in nature, in creation.[5] This makes sense, of course, because Jesus is the firstborn of all creation, in whom all things came into being. Jesus is the incarnation, God made flesh, and he shared particles and atoms and breath and dust with the whole of the created world. That world is groaning, and Jesus is intimately connected to it: "The human Jesus—whose origin was forged with the stars and the amoebas and whose elements and possibilities are also ours . . . prophetically proclaimed the reign of God's shalom. . . . [His] ministry of healing, feeding, and idol-smashing extends to the whole web of life."[6] The New

5. Woodley, *Shalom,* 47. Of course, Jesus knew his audience was a pastoral people, but they probably knew what a wagon was.

6. Fernandez, *Reimagining the Human,* 177–78.

Testament writers make it clear that God will reconcile the world to God's self in time. We understand that we are connected to the earth and to one another, thus the continued importance of and emphasis on community in the early church.

The bitter irony of climate change is that it profoundly and catastrophically impacts those who hold the least responsibility for its advent and have the least power to mitigate its effects. Most ecotheologies point out that creation care is a justice issue, that the poor are disproportionately impacted by climate change, and that those who use the most resources are usually farthest away from the immediate consequences of their consumption. Environmental racism—putting polluting factories in predominantly poor communities of color—is an established reality. Floods, mudslides, hurricanes, earthquakes, and other natural disasters, made more extreme by human activity, have the deadliest impact in the Global South. Indigenous populations who depend on healthy and diverse local ecosystems suffer first and longest when climate change and corrupt public and corporate policies fundamentally alter rivers, lakes, soil, and air.

Brazilian theologian Leonardo Boff, who has watched that country's rainforests, rivers, and indigenous peoples be threatened by dangerous policies and systems fueled by greed, points out that "one-fifth of [Earth's] population is travelling in the passenger section. They consume 80 percent of the supplies for the journey. The other four-fifths are travelling in the cargo hold . . . the most threatened creatures are not whales but the poor, who are condemned to die before their time."[7]

Animals Are Created, Too

Boff argues that "the very same logic of the prevailing system of accumulation and social organization that leads to the exploitation of workers also leads to the pillaging of whole nations and ultimately to the plundering of nature."[8] But despite this deep connection, he goes on to claim that social justice between humans must exist at a minimal level before we can start to work for ecological justice.[9] This seems to miss the point of *kyriarchy*, of the nature of intersecting oppressions, in which one cannot fully understand

7. Boff, "Trinity as Good News for the Poor," 111.

8. Ibid., 110–11.

9. Ibid., 112.

or correct one system of oppression without understanding and correcting those that buttress, interact with, and perpetuate it.

The propensity to put "human concerns" first is strong but misguided. Eleazar Fernandez calls this "naturism" and says it is "a way of thinking and dwelling that places the human species at the top of a hierarchy in which other species are relegated to the status of objects to be exploited."[10] Like Boff, Fernandez sees intersecting oppressions, but rather than put human problems first, Fernandez claims that the struggle for justice for the poor, for women, for people of color, and for other marginalized groups is inseparable from the struggle for eco-justice.[11] Deeply intertwined oppressions cannot be prioritized, because the same privileged mindset of "might makes right" is at the root of all. Attempting to dismantle one oppression alone is futile and might only serve to isolate marginalized groups from one another, thus keeping their creative resistance and power dispersed. Imagine the transformative power of marginalized groups united together and reforming the shape of society to include *all* of those on the margins *and* the dominant center (because they also need to be reconciled to one another, to those they have oppressed, and to God).

This worldview and approach to transformation is theocentric rather than anthropocentric or biocentric. Modern anthropocentric views neglect the centrality of God's continued role in creation. Naturism is an anthropocentric worldview, and it has failed to recognize that "the fundamental ontological distinction lay not between humans and nonhumans, but between God and everything else—God's creation."[12] This failure fuels interpretations of the charge to steward the earth as one of vertical dominion, where humans are above and differentiated from *all* of the rest of creation.[13] One antidote to the damage caused by an entirely vertical view of the human relationship with and position in creation is to acknowledge and adopt the presence of "fellow-creatureliness," demonstrated throughout the scriptures.[14]

Here I can hear my good friend and mentor Ron Sider reminding me that it is humans who are uniquely made in the image of God, and it is humans who have been specially charged with caring for the earth and its

10. Fernandez, *Reimagining the Human*, 160.

11. Ibid., 164.

12. Yordy, *Green Witness*, 20.

13. Bauckham, "Stewardship and Relationship," 103.

14. Bauckham, *Living with Other Creatures*, 153.

inhabitants. But unique does not equal superior. Special privilege does not equal free rein. God's covenant is with every living creature. "Before God the Creator we and our descendants and all living things are partners in the same covenant. Nature is not our property . . . All living beings are partners in God's covenant, each in its own way."[15] God created nonhuman animals with their own specialness. Each individual has a personality, needs, and desires. Each species has a natural way of being and interacting with other created beings. But because we like the taste of flesh, the feel of fur, or the thrill of seeing a wild animal up close, we have chosen groups of species within this vast creation and decided that they are "ours," and it is having a devastating effect on the environment.

Developing a Holistic Ethic of Creation Care

So, how do we establish a holistic ethic of creation care—one that acknowledges the image of God in us but refrains from falling into patterns of destruction that have oppressed the poor and led to a global ecological crisis? While a variety of the ways we have decided to use animals has deleterious effects on the environment (taking native species from their habitats to shove into zoos alters local ecosystems, as does trapping wild animals for their fur), this section will focus primarily on using animals for food, as the global impacts of raising and killing tens of billions of animals is, frankly, astonishing.

A Look at What Is

MEAT WASTES ESSENTIAL WATER AND GRAIN

In 2011, in the United States, we consumed 26.5 billion pounds of cow flesh.[16] In 2012, in the United States, we consumed 35.4 billion pounds of chickens and turkeys[17] and nearly 18 billion pounds of pigs.[18] Since it takes upward of sixteen pounds of grain to produce a single pound of flesh and two thousand gallons of water to produce a single gallon of milk, that means

15. Moltmann, "God's Covenant and Our Responsibility," 111.

16. U.S. Department of Agriculture Economic Research Service, "U.S. Beef Industry," table 1, line 10.

17. Ibid., "Total Poultry," 4–5.

18. Ibid., "Pork: Supply," 5.

billions upon billions of pounds of grain and gallons of water were pumped into animals to produce a limited and costly food source for an already fattened populace instead of being distributed directly to hungry, thirsty people throughout the world. The World Health Organization reports that "chronic food deficits affect about 792 million people in the world, including 20 percent of the population in developing countries. Worldwide, malnutrition affects one in three people and each of its major forms dwarfs most other diseases globally."[19]

Global food production is high enough to feed every man, woman, and child on the planet. But a *huge* percentage of what we grow is pumped into animals, and we get a fraction of caloric energy in return. The image on the following page, created by PETA, helped put the situation into perspective for me.

---

19. World Health Organization, "Water-Related Diseases," par. 7.

FEEDING THE FUTURE

As the world's population continues to multiply, it is now more important than ever to examine the impact that our food choices have on others.

How can we possibly feed 7 billion people?

A renewed sense of responsibility and altruism is a good start.

Wasted Resources, Wasted Lives

Animals raised for food currently take up 30% of the Earth's entire land surface

Livestock Grazing

- threatens native plant species
- leads to soil erosion and eventual desertification
- renders once-fertile land barren

The Broken Link in Our Food Chain

16 lbs. of grain can...

GRAIN 16 LB.

be fed to a cow

or

be fed directly to humans

which will provide just 1/3 of daily caloric needs of just one person.

and meet the caloric needs of up to 10 people for a day.

60% of the world's grain is fed to farmed animals.

Meanwhile, 925 million people do not have enough to eat.

925,000,000

Because No One Should Go Thirsty

Approximately 884 million people lack access to clean water.

That's more than the populations of the USA, Canada and the European Union combined.

Water Needed to Produce

Water Used in Meat and Soy Production in 2009

5 trillion gallons

235 trillion gallons

1 lb. of meat = 2,400 gallons

1 lb. of wheat = 155 gallons

Are you outraged by our current food system?
Take a stand: Go vegan.

PeTA

Here are some additional facts:

- Half of the world's greenhouse gas emissions are attributable to animals raised for food.[20]

- It takes at least thirteen pounds of grain plus another thirty pounds of grasses to produce just a pound of meat.[21]

- You want a pound of animal protein? That requires one hundred times more water than a pound of plant protein.

- Up to five thousand gallons of water are required for every pound of beef.[22]

The Global North is often accused of using far more than its fair share of resources. We vow to change the kind of light bulbs we use, drive a little less, take reusable shopping bags to the grocery store, recycle our pizza boxes and water bottles . . . These are all valuable changes, but they barely make a dent when we continue to chow down on animals.

In the first chapter of Genesis, God prescribes a vegan diet for human and nonhuman animals alike and calls the created world "very good" (Gen 1:29–31). In the second account of the creation story, God tells the human creatures to "till and keep" the garden (Gen 2:15). We are tilling the garden, but we aren't doing a very good job of keeping it. In the United States about 60 percent of our pastures are overgrazed, and soil erosion is accelerating at an unsustainable pace.[23] The land simply isn't meant to sustain billions of people relying on a diet of animal products.

It would be bad enough if we were wreaking this havoc just on our own soil, but globalization has exported more than cheap and dangerous clothing manufacturing to the majority world. In an effort to keep pace with the global market and capitalize on an export market hungry for animal protein, the cattle industry in the Brazilian Amazon has become, according to Greenpeace, the "largest driver of deforestation in the world, responsible for an average of one acre lost every eight seconds."[24] Greenpeace researchers found that in the 2004–2005 growing season alone, 2.9 million

20. Maisto, "Eating Less," par. 3.

21. Pimentel and Pimentel, "Sustainability of Meat-Based and Plant-Based Diets," 662S.

22. Ibid.

23. Ibid.

24. Greenpeace International, "Slaughtering the Amazon," 3.

acres of rainforest were destroyed to raise crops used to feed animals on factory farms.[25] Meanwhile, Oxfam reports that sixty-six million Brazilians face daily food insecurity.[26] This is just one example of the global failures of today's food production methods.

Cows

The environmental devastation caused by eating animals would be bad enough on its own. But we are perpetuating cycles of cruelty while we trample and destroy the planet on which we live. Since many folks equate global warming with cow farts, we will talk about cows briefly here. But the fact is that our mass breeding of cows is just a part of the overall problem.

Cows raised and killed for their flesh and skin are taken from their mothers when they are a few hours old. They are castrated, their horns are cut out of their heads, and their tails are cut off, all without any pain relief. Calves who are sick or lame, or who become injured, are beaten to death or shot. Cows raised for their flesh *may* be able to graze for a time on grasses and prairies, but to "finish" them, they are taken to a barren feedlot and given a high-calorie diet. Within two years, cows bred for their flesh are hanging upside down on a chain by one leg while their throats are slit open. They may or may not be dead when workers on a slaughterhouse line start to hack off their hooves and rip the skin from their backs.

Female calves are used for the dairy industry. Using a "rape rack," they are repeatedly impregnated. Their babies are taken from them shortly after birth because, as mammals, mother cows make milk to feed their babies. Humans are the only species to regularly drink milk after infancy, and the only species to drink the milk of another species. We have chosen cows' milk, a substance designed to nourish a baby cow into a two-thousand-pound adult within a year. Makes perfect sense, right?

Neighbors of dairy farms in California report that the cries of mother cows can be heard for days after their babies are taken. Male calves are tied up in dark crates for sixteen weeks, unable to turn around, walk, or lie down comfortably. Forced to eat, sleep, and defecate in the same small space, these baby boys are sold to slaughter for veal.

Cows used for their milk are kept in massive barns or barren lots. Unnaturally forced to produce far more milk than normal, their udders

25. Greenpeace, "Go Vegetarian," par. 7.
26. Kilpatrick, "Fighting Hunger," par. 3.

become badly infected (mastitis). You might not have known this, but there is an amount of pus and blood in cow's milk that the government has decided is allowable.

Because they are kept on hard surfaces and are unable to walk or graze naturally, cows used for their milk frequently become lame. Called "downed cows," these gentle mothers are prodded into auction with electric shocks or beatings. If they are unable to walk into the slaughterhouse, they are dragged with forklifts, pushed with backhoe loaders, or hauled by a tractor and chains. Sometimes, they are simply left to slowly die at the edge of a property. No cow used for her milk is retired to a lush pasture at the end of her milk-producing days. Her used-up body is sold for hamburger or pet food. A cow's natural life span is fifteen to twenty years. In the United States, most cows are dead before they are four or five. Stories about cows escaping trucks bound for slaughter, running away from the slaughter line, searching for their babies, or experiencing life for the first time outside of a dark warehouse are abundant. Cows want to live, want to be with their families, and jump for joy when given a chance.

What Ought to Be: Shalom

Shalom is the concept of right relationships, not just between humans, but between all elements of God's creation. When we think about shalom, we might envision the perfect harmony of Eden and the promise of full restoration through Jesus that marks the kingdom of God. Shalom is flourishing, and it is for all of God's creation. Woodley reminds us that "shalom, with its embedded concern for the poor, the marginalized, the animals, the birds, the earth, etcetera, is the divinely preferred way for humans to live."[27]

If our lives now were marked by shalom, we might all be able to see chickens this way:

> If we had the mind of Christ, however, and saw these creatures as having a role in God's new creation, we would think about what we can do to make sure that our relationships with chickens contributed to their nurture, health and even delight. Because Christ is the one through whom and for whom the whole world is created, chickens are part of his renewing ministry that leads all creatures into the fullness of life. Inspired and shaped by Christ's reconciling life, we

27. Woodley, *Shalom*, 80.

must concern ourselves with the well-being of animals, working to make sure that they can live the life God intends for them.[28]

Unfortunately, nice sentiments like the one above about nonhuman animals and other created beings—sentiments typical of a green theology—are usually followed by things like this: "The creatures we eat and those we eat with can be assured that our desire abides in God's desire that all creatures taste the heavenly delight that daily creates and sustains the world."[29] I cannot imagine the church praising God and thanking a woman for the use of her body while she was being raped; I cannot imagine that the church's expression of gratitude for the products made by enslaved labor would somehow ease that terrible human suffering. These illogical leaps seem to exist simply to allow humans to continue to use and abuse animal bodies.

We can learn a lot about shalom and fellow-creatureliness from Job. In the midst of his suffering, Job saw some sense in creation:

> But ask the animals, and they will teach you;
> the birds of the air, and they will tell you;
> ask the plants of the earth, and they will teach you;
> and the fish of the sea will declare to you.
> Who among all these does not know
> that the hand of the LORD has done this?
> In his hand is the life of every living thing
> and the breath of every human being. (Job 12:7–10)

When God responds to Job and Elihu, it is with an extensive portrait of God as creator and sustainer. Read Job 38 and 39. This is not a God who has exited the world, who has set it on a course and moved on to other things. Ours is a God so intimately familiar with creation that God sees when mountain goats and deer crouch to give birth. And God reminds Job that the hawk soars because of God's wisdom, not the wisdom of human beings. God is creator, God is sustainer, God is reconciler of *all things*. Fernandez echoes God in Job 39:26 when he says, "If by superiority we mean

---

28. Wirzba, "Reconciliation through Eating," 120–21.

29. Ibid., 134. Eleazar Fernandez calls for something similar when he says, "We need to tell our children that every time we eat ham, beefsteak, and lamb stew, we are eating pig, cow, and sheep. . . . It is only in this manner that we can celebrate and enjoy our eating" (*Reimagining the Human*, 163).

that everybody and everything depends on us, we have failed to understand the web of relationship."[30]

Moving from Is to Ought

Can I tell you how crazy it makes me to open a book on creation care and read about recycling and hybrid cars but not about the resource-intensive meat and dairy industries? In a random survey of books on ecotheology or creation care from an evangelical perspective, only two of them mentioned reducing dependence on animal flesh as a way to reconcile with and help protect creation. None advocated for exclusively plant-based diets. Instead, readers are encouraged to change their light bulbs, use recycled paper, buy energy-efficient appliances, remodel for energy efficiency, protect wildlife habitats, turn off the lights when not in use, bicycle to church, and take shorter showers. Many (too many) of the suggestions were available only to those who were already in positions of privilege. One author claimed, "Humans have a moral responsibility to sustain the order of the world God created,"[31] but neglected to mention that God made the world vegetarian. Another book incorrectly argued that God "set things up so that creatures would have to eat other creatures in order to live."[32] Uh . . . no, please see Genesis 1. I am afraid that until theologians and practitioners start connecting the dots between planetary devastation and our view of animals, calls for a green revolution in the church will ring pretty hollow.

"Christians can only encounter other creatures as other people; each creature is a being for whom Christ died in order to take it up into the reconciliation of the world . . . None of these other creatures is destined to be material for human technology and manipulation."[33] If we wish to live a life reflective of the interpenetrating, interdependent Trinitarian perichoresis, if we wish to care for this creation, then we cannot live as dominators, as rulers, or even as overseers. Instead, we must live in mutual submission and devotion.

---

30. Fernandez, *Reimagining the Human*, 173.

31. Clifford, "Ecological Lament," 59.

32. Brown, *Our Father's World*, 59.

33. Moltmann, *Creating a Just Future*, 67.

---
 15 ---

Can You Be a Peace-Loving Meat-Eater?
(PSSST, NO, 'CAUSE USING ANIMALS NECESSITATES VIOLENCE)

Teaching Empathy to Michael Vick

IN EARLY SEPTEMBER 2007, I was called into a meeting at PETA and given
a top-secret project. NFL quarterback Michael Vick, who had been in-
dicted earlier that year on dogfighting and conspiracy charges, was going
to spend a day at PETA. A federal investigation had revealed that Vick had
bankrolled a dogfighting operation run on his property in Surry County,
Virginia, just a short drive from PETA's headquarters in Norfolk. I was
charged with the development of a daylong course in empathy for animals.
For two weeks, I compiled and modified PETA curriculum to suit the task
at hand, and I developed an exam to measure whether or not the messages
from the day had sunk in.

On the day Vick came to the office, we held a series of short lectures
and discussions, watched a horrific video about the connection between
cruelty to animals and other criminal behavior, studied the Bible, and ate
lunch together. All of the activities were designed to help Vick hone in on
a sense of empathy for animals, to learn to put himself in their shoes. At
the end of the day, I gave him the final exam, graded it, and then sent him
a certificate of completion (yes, he passed). By November of that year, Vick
was in prison, serving a twenty-three-month sentence. The federal investigation revealed that in addition to funding the dogfighting operation—in
which dozens, if not hundreds, of dogs had been injured or killed—Vick
had a direct hand in the deaths of losing dogs. Dogs who lost or who were
unable to fight were electrocuted, drowned, hung, and sometimes beaten

to death. The search of Vick's property revealed carcasses and skeletons of numerous dogs.

While some fans remained loyal, the popular consensus was that what he had done was simply unforgiveable. A friend of mine recently shared that when Vick was arrested, her brother auctioned off his Vick jersey in a yard sale and donated the proceeds to their local animal shelter. Vick was utterly reviled by millions that year, and he continues to be unpopular with folks who describe themselves as "dog lovers." PETA even got flak for welcoming him into the office and attempting to teach him a different way of relating.

But here's a sticky problem: how mad can you get at someone for killing animals if you yourself pay someone to kill animals for you?

I felt the same disconnect when I was helping organize a summit of evangelicals to discuss proactive peacemaking, just war, and nonviolence. My half-joking suggestion that we consider that peace begins on our plates and serve only vegetarian meals was kindly but firmly rejected. So, as I sat in the summit a few months later, watching my fellow Jesus-following peacemakers chow down on animals during lunch, I wrote the piece below.[1]

What bothered me that day during lunch was this: raising and killing animals for food meets no one's criteria for the justified use of violence, when the victims are humans. The just war proponents who were present at the summit would have argued that it was wrong to perpetuate violence on the innocent, since the use of violence requires a just cause, and that violence must be measured with as much mercy as possible. Meanwhile, the nonviolent peacemakers and pacifists argued vehemently that violence was not a solution to any problem and pointed to the nonviolent way of Jesus as our example to emulate. But both camps fail to apply their own principles to created beings who look and sound different than they do.

PEACE BEGINS ON OUR PLATES

At least three times a day, we have the opportunity to choose non-violence. We don't have to face down an enemy carrying a gun, brave counter-protestors, or venture into danger to do so. We can simply pick plants over animals.

---

1. "Peace Begins on Our Plates," originally published in the January/February 2013 issue of *PRISM Magazine*, a publication of Evangelicals for Social Action. Reprinted with permission.

At least three times a day, we have the opportunity to choose mercy over suffering. While we're praying and striving for peace, pursuing reconciliation, confessing our many shortcomings, and drowning in the midst of a million things that we can't control, we can choose corn instead of chicken.

At least three times a day, we can exercise holy dominion, instead of human dominion. Human dominion is power over, for selfish gain. God's dominion is reconciliation with, for wholeness and peace. We can choose tofu instead of turkey.

At least three times a day, we can use our whole bodies to promote peace. Because how much sense does it make to speak and work for the Prince of Peace in one breath, and gnaw on the corpse of a tortured, mutilated animal in the other? We can choose peas instead of pigs.

At least three times a day, we can live out our love of neighbor. Because why should our idea of neighbor end at our block, our city, our nation, our faith, our species? We can choose barley over bacon.

At least three times a day, we can choose empathy, compassion, and justice, qualities that are set aside when we nonhuman animals dehumanize one another to justify war, violence, and oppression.

Evangelicals point to William Wilberforce as a peacemaking hero, one who worked doggedly to end the slave trade in England, as a direct outpouring of his love for God and his faith. We rarely mention that Wilberforce was also a founding member of the Royal Society for the Prevention of Cruelty to Animals. He was deeply concerned with the humane treatment of nonhuman animals. Recognizing the qualities that allow us to stand in solidarity with and care for those who are weak and persecuted, we can choose to embrace those qualities with our whole lives simply by choosing wheat instead of meat.

The violence endured by nonhuman animals is systemic, sustained, and on a scale that is nearly impossible to comprehend. In the U.S. alone, twenty-seven billion nonhuman animals are killed each year for food. They are bred, born, and raised in conditions that deny every God-given natural instinct. Chickens and turkeys have their beaks seared off when they are days old. Cows and pigs have their teeth cut out, their tails cut off, and are castrated without pain relief. Cow's horns are gouged out of their heads. After living cramped in mud, feces, and filth, they are thrown into crates or prodded onto trucks for a long and terrifying trip to a slaughterhouse, where they are hung upside down and their throats are slit. Many are still alive and able to feel pain when slaughterhouse workers begin to rip the skin or feathers from their bodies. Every minute of their miserable lives is marked by violence.

At least three times a day, we can remind ourselves that the kingdom of God has been here, is here now manifested in the Holy Spirit, and will be here again. We live in the tension of the already and the not yet. While evangelicals are increasingly abandoning the idea that "this world is not my home" and instead working in any small capacity to make this home more accurately reflect that kingdom ideal, let's remember that our image of what the world *should* and, more importantly, *can* look like is found in Genesis 1 and 2. It is peaceful. It is nonviolent. It is the whole of creation fully reconciled to God and one another. It is a world without death, including the death of nonhuman animals. It is a vegetarian world.

Basic Arguments for Nonviolence

In chapter 5, we talked about christological power and how that looked different to first-century Palestinian Jews than they had expected it to. In this chapter, we will look at the basic, Jesus-centered arguments for nonviolence. If you are a diehard just war theorist and believe firmly that it is okay for humans to kill one another, this section may not convince you otherwise, but I hope that you will consider whether or how killing animals fits in your ethical framework as it relates to the acceptable uses of violence. It seems to me that those who advocate for just war could only really justify violence against nonhuman animals if they or someone else were in mortal danger, and I just cannot for the life of me recall the last time someone was killed by a rampaging chicken.

Walter Wink's Third Way of Nonviolent Engagement

One account of the nonviolent way of Jesus has been offered by Walter Wink, who argues that Jesus's commands in Matthew 5:38–43 (to turn the other cheek, to give your cloak, and to go the second mile) were not calls for passivity in the face of oppression but for proactive nonviolent resistance. Wink argues that the verb "to resist" has been incorrectly translated and that the Greek word used in the passage (*antistēnai*) should be read as "to resist *violently.*" In other words, Jesus's famous call is not for recipients of evil to lie down and take it but to engage in creative, nonviolent opposition that liberates both the dominated and dominator from the tyranny of oppression.[2]

The Transforming Initiatives of the Sermon on the Mount

When I first learned about the Sermon on the Mount, it was presented as a series of lofty ideals. Who can avoid anger? Or lust? Influenced by Wink and other scholars and practitioners, Stassen and Gushee offer an alternative structure. The authors reframe fourteen teachings from Matthew 5:21—7:6 to show that Jesus was offering a way out of the vicious cycle that was so often the result of traditional righteousness through the use of creative initiatives with the power to transform individuals and communities. For instance, rather than allow anger to fester, Jesus teaches that even if we are at the altar, offering praise and sacrifice to God, we are to *leave* and be reconciled with our enemies. It is more important to right relationships than it is to fulfill the obligations of the law. The potential power of this movement toward shalom cannot be overstated. The action "transforms the person who was angry into an active peacemaker; it transforms the relationship from one of anger into a peacemaking process; and it hopes to transform the enemy into a friend. Furthermore, it participates in the way of grace that God took in Jesus when there was enmity between God and humans: God came in Jesus to make peace."[3]

The Violence of Love[4]

I was not even two years old when Archbishop Óscar Romero was gunned down by an assassin in El Salvador, and his legacy did not begin to impact me until years later, when I watched the Hollywood adaptation of his life in a high school classroom during a South and Central American History class. So, my first introduction to Archbishop Romero was as a historico-political figure. Nearly two decades later, at a seminary outside of Philadelphia, I would meet Romero the theologian and my heart would be transformed.

---

2. Walter Wink has written extensively about this, but I drew on his *Engaging the Powers*, 175–93.

3. Stassen and Gushee, *Kingdom Ethics*, 135.

4. I take this section title from a compilation of Romero's homilies by the same name: Óscar Romero, *The Violence of Love*.

In his three years as archbishop of San Salvador, Romero became a strong ally for that country's impoverished and oppressed majority. I just want to share a few passages from Romero's homilies with you:

September 25, 1977

Let us not tire of preaching love; it is the force that will overcome the world. Let us not tire of preaching love. Though we see that waves of violence succeed in drowning the fire of Christian love, love must win out; it is the only thing that can.[5]

July 23, 1978

A merciful God, today's reading calls him. Your sovereignty over all makes you pardon all. You govern us with great indulgence because you can do all that you want to do. It would seem to be the other way around . . . you could treat us cruelly . . . But only God can do whatever he wants, and this God governs us with kindness. In a weak person, power becomes cruelty; a sense of inferiority is carried to the level of brutishness. God has no sense of inferiority. God is sovereign. God can do all, and so he judges even his felons, even his sinners, with kindness and mercy.[6]

November 27, 1977

The violence we preach is not the violence of the sword, the violence of hatred. It is the violence of love, of brotherhood, the violence that wills to beat weapons into sickles for work.[7]

Facing a violent government determined to maintain the status quo, Romero preached a response of love based on the example of the incarnated God, one who grants mercy when none is deserved and who demonstrates kindness to the rich and poor, sick and healthy, young and old, in and out.

Animal Liberation as a Witness to Peace

Can we worship a God who limited Godself to human form, who counted among his inner circle prostitutes, thieves, tax collectors, and outcasts, and who suffered a humiliating death on the cross—while we strip clean

---

5. Romero, *Violence of Love*, 7.

6. Ibid., 63–64.

7. Ibid., 12.

a chicken wing? Can we worship a God who called the peaceful creation "good" and who promises to reconcile the whole earth to shalom, to a state of flourishing and peace—while we gnaw on a pig's rib? Can we claim to follow the Prince of Peace with feet shod in the skin of a cow? Can those of us who work for justice, liberation, and peace do so with bellies full of dead animals? Or can we see the incredible disconnect here between our claimed ethics and practice?

When we chew on animal flesh, we embrace violence. There is no way to use animals in the ways that we do without violence. We use "rape racks" to breed animals; we electrocute and beat them to coerce them into movement; we slam or hoist their unwilling bodies into crates, cages, pens, trucks, and slaughter lines. We amputate, bolt, cut, castrate, dissect, dock, declaw, debeak, dehorn, de-tail, de-feather, drown, decapitate, force-feed, inject, insert, rip, starve, shock, slap, scream at, screw, trap, throw, and whip their bodies until our needs are met, our tastes satisfied, our greed satiated.

Laura Yordy argues that Christ's peace is "the unity of Christ: all things (*ta panta*) united in their source, savior, and destiny . . . This peace is not only interpersonal, but interspecies: not the wary tolerance of animals forced to share a waterhole, but shared communion with God."[8] Our exploration of the prophetic scriptures supports this view. Adopting a praxis of fellow-creatureliness toward animals is a witness to the peace and reconciliation of Christ not only to fellow believers and to the creatures we avoid abusing and killing but also to nonbelievers. For many years, I was the only evangelical Christian working in PETA's campaigns department. My coworkers and I would spend hours watching some new undercover investigation, or hear about some new method of abuse, or see that yet another church was hosting a pig-pickin', and they would turn to me in wonder and ask *why*. Why would people who claim to worship a God of compassion be so cruel? And I would have no answer.

8. Yordy, *Green Witness*, 103.

— 16 —

Whose Bodies Matter?

I NEVER THOUGHT MUCH about what it meant to be made in God's image, most likely because I never personally felt that I qualified for such an honor, having struggled with my weight and general awkwardness since puberty. I have continued throughout adulthood to feel like a visitor in my own skin, maintaining my own brand of body-soul dualism, neglecting or ignoring my body in favor of expanding my mind, and mentally berating myself when my modest and isolated efforts at physical health and wellness fail.

This mind *over* matter mentality is the result of a deeply embedded theological understanding of the world as one made up of hierarchy, a ladder from the dirty muck of the earth to the pure clouds of heaven, which facilitates a narrow and singularly focused view of humanity's mission in the world: "I must reach the top." Here's how it might go: God is "up there." God is good. I am "down here." Down here is bad. I am bad. As a result, "[the dualistic, hierarchical relationship of God and the world] encourages not only an understanding of salvation as the escape of individuals to the spiritual world, but also justifies lack of attention to the flourishing of this world."[1] It is a mentality that separates us from one another, from God, our Creator, and from God's creation, while we thoroughly abuse anyone or anything on the ladder's lower rungs and simultaneously grab for higher rungs at any cost.

I thought understanding the damage caused by that hierarchical thinking to other created beings was all I needed to know in order to begin to live in right relationship, but this language of dominance in relationality is important beyond providing a context for examining how I and other

1. McFague, "Untitled Essay," 85.

humans relate to what is outside of our embodied selves. This embedded language prevents me from experiencing God's reconciling shalom even within my own being. "It is God's nature to be embodied,"[2] but it is hard to imagine God engaged in the same kind of emotional gymnastics related to being an embodied person that I have performed. I am only beginning to wrestle with the implications of this idea for my inner life, and while I do not know what God will reveal to me in the course of this exploration, I do know that I can take a cue from Hagar, for whom survival and success came from communing with God, neither trampling on anyone else nor being trampled on.[3]

Veganism and Human Bodies

When I first went vegan, I lost seventy pounds in six months. My cholesterol dropped nearly one hundred points, and I was able to stop taking antidepressants. I was unrecognizable to people who had known me for years. I felt strong and confident. There were times that I even felt beautiful. But that confidence and serenity did not come from a diet change alone. This period of time in my life was tumultuous and I found myself utterly dependent on God and on the people God placed in my life, a makeshift community spread across the U.S. who blessed me with gifts great and small. Prayer, dependence on others, and fueling my body and brain with life-giving, plant-based nutrients all played a role in that transformative season.

A few more years passed by before I realized that I was far from having it all figured out. My weight managed to yo-yo on a plant-based diet, just as it had on one consisting mainly of animal products. My subpar brain chemistry made itself known again and again. I struggled with feelings of isolation, of loneliness, of despair, of self-loathing, of significant inadequacy. I was deeply envious of my vegan friends who had lithe, slender bodies and who seemed easily happy. Looking back, I can see that having achieved some measure of financial and physical security, I spent less time in fervent prayer, less time humbling myself to ask for help, and had a misplaced sense of confidence in my own ability to achieve and succeed. Even today, I feel constantly at war with myself, knowing that I am utterly dependent on God for everything in life, but acting as if I rule my own world. While I no longer consume animal bodies, I repeatedly fail to fully enter the perichoretic

2. Ibid., 110.

3. Williams, *Sisters in the Wilderness*, 109.

community of creation; instead, I set my own daily course, fooling myself into believing that I am an independent actor and spending so much time thinking and talking that I leave no room to hear God.

Plant-based diets lower cholesterol, lower the risk of heart disease, diabetes, cancer, and stroke. Plant-based diets improve our sleep quality, reduce gastrointestinal distress and disease, and clear our skin. Healthy plant-based diets provide all the nutrients that our bodies need, whether we are couch potatoes or ultra-marathoners.[4] But when people tell me they are vegan for health reasons, I have to stop myself from rolling my eyes. I am thrilled, of course, that fewer animals are being eaten, and I know a few people have made the initial leap to plant-based diets for their own health and stayed the course because they learned the horrifying facts about cruelty inherent in the production of animal foods. But I fear that a good choice made for the wrong reasons leaves the door open for a reversal later on.

Perhaps the latest fad in nutrition calls for a daily diet composed almost entirely of animal protein, or says that the key to losing thigh fat is to eat fish at every meal. Or maybe we dive into the abundance of God's creation and live that out by becoming "foodies" or "adventurous eaters" willing to try anything once. Maybe we fall into the hipster trap of putting bacon on every.freaking.thing.

When we think about and value our own bodies over all others, we miss the point.

Though I still have much to learn about human relationality and I still struggle to practice what I preach, the biblical visions for redemption remain "staggeringly inclusive . . . they speak of . . . a time of universal shalom when all creatures will live together in harmonious and joyful community."[5] We are made in the image of a triune God, a God who is relational, who exists in the communion of the Trinity and creates humans "for life in relationships that mirror or correspond to God's own life in relationship."[6] But standing on our ladder, we have corrupted what it means to be made in God's image to give ourselves "divine" permission to trample those we perceive to be beneath us, taking every possible opportunity to exclude others from our special place of dominion. For me, an important step in reflecting

---

4. Seriously, there are a ton of great books out there about how healthy plant-based diets are, from Rip Esselstien's *Engine 2 Diet* to Brendan Brazier's *Thrive* to Joel Furman's *Eat to Live* and more. Check a few out at your local library. You'll be blown away.

5. Migliore, *Faith Seeking Understanding*, 99.

6. Ibid., 141.

God's life in relationship has been to give up meat, not for my own health but as thrice-daily acknowledgment that my body is not the only body that matters. I believe that God wants us to enjoy the bounty of the earth, but feasting joyously on the flesh of another created being no longer fits into that image.

Veganism and Animal Bodies

When people ask me why I went vegan, I explain four things:

1. I learned what happens to animals on factory farms and in slaughterhouses and did not want to support those industries.

2. I learned about the enormous waste and intensive use of resources required by the production of animal-based foods and did not want to contribute to the deterioration of our environment.

3. I learned that children in the Global South did not have enough to eat partly because of my meat habit.

4. I learned that meat is loaded with cholesterol and saturated fat and that it was making me sick.

I fully intended my veganism to be a phase, a passing fancy. I had started and quit enough things throughout my life that I was prepared to fail at yet another resolution. So when people ask me why I stayed vegan, I tell them that once I learned more about the myriad ways we humans have subjugated and tortured animal bodies, I wanted no part of it.

Pigs

On the relationship between human and nonhuman animals, Sallie McFague argues that understanding and appreciating both similarities and differences between human and nonhuman animals is the first step toward living an honest life in relationship with God's creation. Embodied knowing hopefully leads to embodied doing, and acknowledging that "the common creation story helps us to move into a new paradigm for responding to our fellow animals, one in which we appreciate the network of our interdependence with them as well as their real differences from us."[7]

7. McFague, *Body of God*, 119. Human and nonhuman animal relationships are discussed in more depth in 118–24.

So we are going to talk a little bit about pigs.

Pigs. The creatures we draw as cartoons, smiling at us from roadside barbeque joints across the U.S. Not to be a killjoy, but pigs are absolutely not smiling when they are headed to slaughter and they definitely do not want to be your dinner. Pigs. Because their internal anatomy is similar to a human's, they are shot, stabbed, and burned in military trauma and other surgical training exercises (even though there are non-animal methods for trauma training readily available). Pigs. Herded into an enclosed booth and used as live target practice by ammunition and Taser manufacturers.

Pigs are as smart as three-year-old children and smarter than dogs.[8] They have an incredible sense of smell. They love to root, to run, and to play. Google "pigs playing" and watch the videos. They race, leap, and chase one another. Pigs are empathetic. They make friends. They love their babies and communicate through grunts and oinks.[9]

Sick or small or just plain unwanted baby pigs are picked up by farm workers and slammed into the ground. This is a legal form of "euthanasia" for nursing piglets. The American Veterinary Medical Association and the United States Department of Agriculture give this method two hearty thumbs up, because they are primarily interested in protecting the industry status quo, not animals.

Healthy baby pigs are picked up, screaming and writhing, and their tails are cut off, their teeth are cut out, and, if they are baby boys, their testicles are cut off—all without anesthesia or painkiller. On factory farms, they are kept in absolute filth, on slabs of concrete or slatted floors. They eat, sleep, and relieve themselves in the same tiny area. Respiratory infections are common, as is lameness caused by arthritis and other joint problems. Sick and injured pigs are left to die, or they are beaten or shot to death. Pigs are intelligent and naturally very clean. The stress and filth of confinement causes pigs enormous stress, and they vomit frequently.

When they finally reach slaughter weight, they are herded onto trucks and endure long drives through all weather conditions without food or water. More than a million pigs die in transport in the U.S. each year. Hundreds

8. See Angier, "Pigs Prove to Be Smart, if Not Vain."

9. This is why I never say that humans should "give" nonhuman animals a voice or that they are voiceless. They communicate—we just do not usually bother to learn their language. I love the score of the musical *Wicked*, but one of my favorite aspects of the story is that nonhuman animals in their natural state were heard and understood. Only through the intervention of evil did they lose their ability to speak and thus their ability to participate in Oz society.

of thousands more arrive at slaughter crippled, having been crushed in the overcrowded trucks.

Mother pigs, used for breeding, are kept in gestation crates—metal cages no more than two feet wide and not long enough for the pregnant mothers to turn around. Crazy from confinement, these pigs spend hours biting the bars of their cages. When it is time to move the pigs to slightly larger farrowing crates, after they give birth, farmworkers beat the mother pigs with iron posts or boards to force them from one cage to the other.

At the slaughterhouse, pigs are shot in the brain with a captive bolt gun, then hung by their back legs. The bolt gun does not always render pigs unconscious or kill them, and they are frequently alive and able to feel pain as their throats are slit. Many are not dead when they are dumped into scalding water for hair removal.

So, it is pretty easy for me to live without bacon. I bet you could, too.

Every Body Matters

To be a human shaped in the image of God is not a license to trample; it is a mandate to restore. What we must realize is that "creaturehood means radical coexistence, mutual interdependence, rather than solitary or monarchic existence."[10] Moreover, a clearer awareness of ourselves as embodied beings connected to other embodied beings in God's creation allows us to see more fully the christological significance of this physical life. God's incarnation is not only for you or me, or for people who work hard for it, or for people who get all the answers right, or for people who are born into good families, or for white people, or for black people, or for people at all. "We should be able to extend our understanding of God's incarnation to the world of animals and nature around us. God incarnates Godself in the whole cosmos . . . The world is God's incarnation."[11]

The importance of this vision for ministry and its ethical implications are profound. We have to radically reorient ourselves toward and into God's community, which, if you are anything like me, is much larger than what you may be comfortable with. First, we must step off of the ladder and start "tending the garden . . . get busy learning about our neighbors and how we can all live here justly and sustainably."[12] The breath of God that is my spirit

10. Migliore, *Faith Seeking Understanding*, 104.

11. Fernandez, *Reimagining the Human*, 177.

12. McFague, *Body of God*, 114–15.

is the same breath of God that enlivens animals. The flesh and bones in my body are the same flesh and bones in animal bodies. So, rather than asking how we can ensure our own happiness, we can begin to ask how we can bring someone else, no matter their species, into joyful shalom. Let's start by not eating them.

17

Liberate Your Language

IN THIS SHORT CHAPTER, we will start to liberate our language from the phrases that roll off of our tongues but that perpetuate negative stereotypes of God's other creatures. Here goes:

No	Yes
"Kill two birds with one stone."	"See two birds with one telescope," "free two birds with one key," or simply "accomplish two things at once."
"What am I, some guinea pig?"	Avoid normalizing the use of non-human animals in laboratories. Instead, "I'd rather not be your test subject."
"Circus/farm/laboratory animal."	Phrases like "dairy cow" reinforce the (wrong) idea that cows are here for us to use their milk. Instead, say "cow used for milk" or "rhesus monkey used in psychological experiments."
"You're putting the cart before the horse."	"You're putting the car before the engine."

No	Yes
"George has a dog. Its name is Bruiser."	*Her* name is Bruiser. *Her.* Dogs and other nonhuman animals have sex organs and can be identified by a gender pronoun. Please stop using the same pronouns that we use for toasters and sofas to identify living, sentient beings.
"I've been running around like a chicken with my head cut off!"	How about using the more straightforward phrase "My life feels chaotic" or "I've been very busy." Your overbooked schedule is not the same as having your head cut off. I can guarantee it.
"He's dumb as an ox."	There's no alternative for this, simply because it's mean. If you don't have anything nice to say, don't say anything at all.
"She's filthy as a pig."	Ditto above. Also, point of clarification: pigs wallow in mud to cool off. They're really quite clean creatures.
"She's so birdbrained."	And ditto redux.
"We're packed in like sardines."	"We're tightly packed."
"Give a person a fish, they'll eat for a day; teach a person to fish, they'll eat for a lifetime."	Let's just say that education and skills training are vital to human flourishing.
"In my house, I bring home the bacon."	"In my house, I bring home the Benjamins."

No	Yes
"She let the cat out of the bag!"	First, don't put cats in bags. They make carriers for transporting cats. Second, how about this instead: "She spilled the beans!"
"There's more than one way to skin a cat."	I've seen live cats get skinned, and it's horrible. How about "there's more than one way to trim a tree"?
"There's no use beating a dead horse."	Well, it's better to beat a dead horse than a live one. But the saying implies that beating a live horse somehow elicits a positive response. What if we exchanged this awful phrase for "there's no use drinking from an empty cup"?
"Land of milk and honey."	"Paradise."

That's really just the beginning. If you use a phrase often and find that it is a little macabre or speciesist and want help coming up with a better version, hit me up at sarahwithrowking.com.

18

Undercover Investigations:
Hell on Earth Exposed

MOST OF THE CRUELTIES I have described in this book are legal. Awful acts, difficult to read about or watch, but legal. Of course, just because something is legal doesn't mean it's right or good. What we haven't discussed are the obscene cruelties exposed by undercover investigators and whistle-blowers. These men and women pull the curtain back to show the world what really happens on farms, in laboratories, on training grounds, and in any other place where humans exploit animals for profit.

I've been putting off writing this chapter. I know that it's important to take a survey of the relevant cultural and social realities when developing a stance, and to do so, one must overturn the rocks, exposing the muck beneath, but naturally, I'm not all that excited about the emotional and physical toll that painting an effective word portrait of abuse and torture will take. The facts don't need to be embellished; they alone are enough to haunt any compassionate person's thoughts.

I admit that in writing this book, I have at times felt paralyzed by the sheer magnitude of the task, overwhelmed by the many choices I have had to make. When I talk about testing on animals, should I focus on rabbits, whose eyes and skin are used to test mascara and lotion? Should I talk about great apes, whose bodies are injected and dissected for decades? Should I talk about dogs, who are given varying lethal doses of medicine and observed while they die slow, agonizing deaths? Should I talk about mice and rats, who aren't covered by the one federal law that protects animals in labs—although they make up the bulk of animals used—and who are routinely decapitated with scissors? There aren't enough pages in the world to adequately convey the grotesque creativity humans have displayed in their abuse of animals. In our world, no matter what we profess on Sunday, we believe that might gives us the right to do what we want, when we want, to whomever we want.

But there are a couple of important reasons to do the uncomfortable work of exposure, on both our parts. First, undercover investigators who expose the realities for animals are men and women who had to observe abuses firsthand. There's a big difference between reading about someone's suffering and being in the room with them while they suffer. It's a little easier for some folks to distance themselves from the written word. I feel pressed to honor those who have sacrificed their own comfort in order to expose and stop atrocities. And I want us to honor the lives of the animals who have endured misery and pain at human hands.

The second reason is this: I had a friend once who got *suuuuuper* angry at another friend for eating baby cows tied up for four months in dark crates and then slaughtered (veal) and telling us about it. The same friend ate all the other animals, though, so the reaction confused me. Then I remembered that when I would start to mention a video I'd seen at work that day, she'd cover her ears and ask me to stop. She didn't want to know. She was an extremely empathetic person who didn't want to change her habits, so she avoided knowledge that she knew would first pain her and then force her into the unwanted position of having to choose between change and willful participation in systems of cruelty. It's hypocrisy, and I'm as guilty of it as anyone. But rather than throw our hands in the air and declare ourselves helpless, let's face the ugliness together and resolve to urge one another on to compassion.

A lot of folks in the church don't like to engage with discomfort. We don't like to talk about depression, suicide . . . we don't sit in the ashes very often, as a group, and tend to prefer talking about struggle only after that struggle has been tied up in a redemptive bow. Facing the reality of how we use animals today is a dark affair. But face it we must.

In my first nine years at PETA, there were a few undercover investigations that stood out to me, that have haunted my waking thoughts, and that have forever altered how I view humans. It is those experiences that I wish to share now.

Chinese Fur Farms

Watch: http://www.peta.org/issues/animals-used-for-clothing/fur/
chinese-fur-industry/

I will never forget the day I first saw undercover investigation footage of fur farms in China. I sat in a tiny conference room a few feet from my desk at PETA's headquarters on the Elizabeth River in Norfolk, in front of a small television with my boss, our communications director, and a representative from PETA Asia-Pacific who had worked with the investigator.

I saw row upon row of cages filled with pacing, terrified animals. These particular animals were raccoon dogs, members of the *canid* family and indigenous to East Asia. Workers reached into the cages, yanked out dogs one by one and slammed them to the ground. Each dog was bludgeoned until she stopped moving long enough for the worker to flip her onto her back and begin to skin her. Many animals were not dead, and many regained consciousness as their skin was ripped from their flesh. The skinned bodies were thrown onto a pile. I'll never forget the horror and sickness I felt the first time I saw one of those fully skinned dogs slowly raise her head and blink at the camera.

Another investigation revealed that dogs and cats had been crammed into flimsy wire cages and stacked onto trucks for transport to slaughter. The cages were so overcrowded that their limbs would slip through the wires. Despite this, workers stacked cages one on top of the other into trucks and, at the destination, flung them to the concrete ground, smashing and breaking their delicate legs. The dogs and cats were bludgeoned, strung up on wires, and skinned. Fur from dogs and cats in China is frequently used as trim on garments sold in the United States, and years of investigation by the Humane Society of the United States revealed that some garments that were labeled as "faux" fur actually came from dogs and cats in China.

Of course, animals killed for fur here in the U.S. or in Europe don't fare any better. In one undercover investigation, I saw minks yanked from cages and held down as electrodes were placed in their vaginas or anuses. Though it causes excruciating pain prior to death, this kind of electrocution is common because it preserves the animal's fur.

Canadian Seal Hunt

Watch: http://www.youtube.com/watch?v=zw8MKd__1L0

Despite bans on seal fur or seal meat in major markets across the globe, each year the Canadian government issues permits to off-season fisherman to bludgeon and skin hundreds of thousands of seals. Even if the demand for baby seal skin and meat were high, this would be a particularly heinous practice. Here's why.

Each year, pregnant seals gather in Canada to give birth to babies. For a few weeks, these nurseries are peaceful, full of white-coated babies and nursing mothers. Then the hunters arrive. Armed with shotguns and hakapiks (heavy clubs with an iron pick on one end), these hunters (largely of European descent) shoot or bludgeon the babies and mothers as their companions look on helplessly. Some seals try to escape but are unable to outrun the hunters.

Dead and dying seals are hooked with the hakapik and dragged onto ships for skinning. Hunters are supposed to check for signs of life before they rip the skin from the seal's bodies, but this is not always done and one animal welfare group found that 40 percent of the seals were still alive and conscious as they were skinned.[1] Because there is no demand for seal meat, the carcasses are left on the ice to rot. There is *nothing* so horrifying as watching a hunter beat a helpless baby seal to death. I once saw video footage of a small dog being beaten to a literal pulp with a shovel. Even that atrocity was quicker and slightly less awful than the seal slaughter.

Horse Racing

Watch: http://bit.ly/1qYKTl4

One of the last investigations that PETA released before I left for seminary was of speed trials for juvenile thoroughbred horses used by the horse racing industry. During these trials, still developing horses are forced to sprint at breakneck speeds to impress potential buyers. The strain of these races frequently injures the horses. In this particular investigation, while a young female horse was sprinting down the track, her cannon bone broke, the sound like a rocket. In slow motion, you can see fragments of bone shooting from her leg, leaving her foot to dangle helplessly. Despite this

1. Fielder et al., "Veterinary Report," 9.

catastrophic injury, she continues to run, unable to stop her incredible momentum. On a different track, with temperatures soaring over one hundred degrees, a young male horse dropped dead of a burst aorta while being forced to sprint.

These are utterly senseless deaths brought on by the irresponsible actions of a greedy industry. Horses used for racing are pumped full of performance-enhancing drugs, forced to race before their bones and muscles are fully developed, made to run on hard surfaces that damage their joints, whipped, auctioned off to the highest bidder, and finally killed for their meat in filthy slaughterhouses. Yet, like so many other types of animal, we humans intentionally breed horses for lives of misery and terrifying deaths.

Covance

Watch: http://www.peta.org/features/covance-incs-cruel-animal-experimentation/

Have you ever heard a monkey scream in fear? Covance, a contract research corporation, tests products on animals for other companies. For nearly a year, a PETA investigator worked in a Covance laboratory, documenting conditions and violations of basic animal welfare laws there. Monkeys, who are highly social animals, were kept isolated in cages. Technicians hit and screamed at terrified monkeys, who were yanked from their cages only to have tubes shoved down their noses and into their stomachs so that toxic substances could be pumped in. The monkey's screams are sounds I will never forget. Sick and injured monkeys weren't given veterinary care.

There are some products tested on animals over which we may not have control. A medicine that you need in order to survive may have been tested on animals. That doesn't mean you should stop taking the medicine. But the shampoo you use may have also been tested on animals, and it's very easy to find cruelty-free shampoo. It's also important to speak up. When you hear about or see cruelty, when you see a nonhuman animal being treated as an inanimate object . . . say something. Silence only fuels cruelty.

Sun Pet—Supplier for PetSmart and PETCO

Watch: http://bit.ly/1t6il07

From an early age, I was bummed out to see dogs and cats in pet shop windows. They looked kind of sickly and sad. When I learned about puppy mills, I understood that my worry was well founded. But I didn't realize that the smaller animals in the back of the pet shop were just as bad off until one day I was walking through a mall in Birmingham, Alabama. I saw rows and rows of little hamsters in these tiny plastic boxes. One little guy caught my attention. He was trying to climb up the side of his box. I stood there and watched him for what felt like an eternity, his little paws clinging as best as they could to the slippery plastic, his twitching nose and whiskers offering him clues to his escape. He couldn't escape, but he kept trying, again and again and again. My heart broke in that store.

Years later, my heart broke again when we released an undercover investigation of Sun Pet, a small-animal supplier to large chains, including PETCO and PetSmart. The investigator saw one worker put live hamsters into a bag and smash it into a table again and again to kill the animals inside. Other animals were gassed to death in a filthy chamber. Sick and dying animals were not given veterinary care, and conditions in the warehouse were cramped and filthy. Please—never, ever buy an animal. Shelters are teeming with animals small and large to adopt. Buying animals, even shopping at stores that sell live animals, perpetuates the demand for breeders and dealers who make a killing off of cruelty.

These are just a few examples of the investigations that struck a chord in me. It is a sliver of the information available online. Though it is hard, I hope you will resolve to watch a few of these videos on your own and share the information with someone you love.

Now What? The Basics of Treating Animals Well

Introduction to Part Three

MOST OF US GREW up eating meat and drinking milk, buying leather shoes, and going to the zoo. Others hunt, fish, or breed their dog in order to give puppies away to neighbors or make a few bucks. As we realize the impact of our choices and decide to change our behavior, we can feel overwhelmed. Does caring about animals mean you become a granola-eating, soymilk-making, wheatgrass-juicing, patchouli-using hippy? Will we have to eat only twigs and leaves? What if we hate vegetables? What difference can we really make, anyway? For those whom God leads to make a change, this section lays out basic first steps toward a more holistically compassionate life.

I won't lie. It will take a tiny bit of work. But not much, and not more than an everyday person with a family and a job can handle. It won't cost more money. You won't have to join a commune. You won't become a social outcast. Caring about animals doesn't have to become the central focus of your life. And you don't have to label yourself—in fact, I'd urge you *not* to label yourself as an "animal rights person" or a vegan or anything else. The *only* label we have and should care about is that we're children of God. Perhaps by taking these simple steps to reduce your participation in cruelty and suffering, you'll be better able to live into that important label, but in the long view, it doesn't really matter what you call yourself; it matters how you live. How you serve. And how you reflect God's love in a hurting world.

It can be hard to know where to start, though, and so the next few chapters will lay out some steps to take, and some ways that you can answer questions about your new commitment without alienating the folks around you who aren't quite ready to walk with you on this journey.

19

Don't Eat Them

I WENT VEGAN WHILE living in Milton, Florida, a town of about seven thousand people whose main employer, after the Navy, seemed to be a Piggly Wiggly supermarket. It was not a hotbed of animal rights activity and vegan options did not abound at the city's most popular eateries: a Texas Roadhouse and a Captain D's Seafood Kitchen. Happily, just a few miles away in Pensacola, there was a lovely co-op with loads of fresh produce and some vegan alternatives like Tofutti cream cheese and So Delicious ice cream that made the transition pretty painless. I've found that a lot of communities have these little gems. Driving cross-country in 2013, I had a delicious tofu sandwich at a co-op in Billings, Montana. On that same trip, I ate two BK Veggie Burgers with a giant iced tea in Rapid City, South Dakota to the soundtrack of the Sturgis Motorcycle Rally; enjoyed a vegan skillet breakfast and a cup of coffee at a Perkins restaurant in Sioux Falls; and had raw vegan cheese perogies and egg-free spinach quiche in Downers Grove, Illinois.

My point is this: it doesn't matter where you live. Once you decide to stop eating animals, the options are plentiful. I think my palate and plate have dramatically diversified since going vegan in 2002. There are lots of resources for people looking to make the transition from a standard American diet to a healthy, plant-based lifestyle (PETA's is the best: http://www.peta.org/living/food/making-transition-vegetarian/), but here are a few tips that have worked for me:

1. **Pick a few of your favorite recipes and experiment with vegan alternatives to meat and dairy ingredients.** I never wanted a Thanksgiving without my mom's sausage and celery stuffing. Winters were too gloomy without her spaghetti sauce, and Christmas wasn't Christmas

unless the smell of yeasty orange rolls wafted through the house. I've veganized all of these and more.

2. **If you don't have a large family, partner with a friend and buy into a local CSA (community supported agriculture).** Each week, you'll get a load of local produce and, if you're like me, you won't have seen half of it before! Google these new veggies and have fun trying them. Before I tried our local CSA, I thought radishes only came in one variety and they were only served raw, on salads. Turns out, oven-roasted radishes loose their bitterness and become sweet, juicy tidbits of heaven in your mouth.

3. **Take your transition slowly, if that seems right for you.** Once I decided to go vegan, I ate the non vegan food that I had in my house and simply didn't buy any more animal-based foods. You might want to cut out one animal at a time. There's no right or wrong way to start living a more compassionate life. Just get on with it.

4. **Resolve to reduce suffering where you can, when you can.** So many friends of mine have come to me forlorn when they failed to practice their ethics. More often, people don't even begin new practices because they're afraid of failure. I admit that I have slipped over the course of the last twelve years, even though most days it seems that the force of my convictions keeps my heart pumping and my lungs moving air. There's no perfect way to be. As Christians, we know that it's impossible to attain perfection on earth. To me, that's a convicting comfort. I can throw guilt and shame out the door (or try to, at least) and live the love I've been given, knowing I won't always do that well. Changing the *whole world* is an impossible task. And it's supposed to be impossible for humans. But when each one of us simply resolves to reduce suffering where we can, choices become clearer and the task of living in a broken world seems a bit more manageable.

Here are a few free websites with recipes that I really like:

*   http://ohsheglows.com/: healthy and delicious food, period.

*   http://www.meettheshannons.com/: Annie and Dan are hysterical, sweet, and genuinely interested in helping you "eat to win."

*   http://blog.fatfreevegan.com/: Susan feeds her kid and hubby on the food she features in the blog, and I've yet to discover a dud recipe in

the mix. Her green bean casserole recipe is now a holiday staple in our house.

If you're wanting information on the health impacts of going vegan, I highly recommend these resources:

- Physician's Committee for Responsible Medicine—http://www.pcrm.org/

- The Vegetarian Resource Group—http://www.vrg.org/ (I do not like their website, but they do have *tons* of great information, you just have to be patient getting it.)

- Vegan Bodybuilding and Fitness—http://www.veganbodybuilding.com/ (Show these pics to the haters!)

- Vegan Outreach—http://www.veganhealth.org/ (This is another not-super-slick website, but one with good solid information.)

If you decide you have other questions on this journey, feel free to drop me a line at sarahwithrowking.com/about.

20

Don't Beat Them

(OR PAY PEOPLE WHO DO)

A Short List of Dos:

1. **Enjoy animals in their own environments.** If you're not in the 1 percent and can't go on a photographic safari, look up some of the amazing programming available from the BBC, National Geographic, and others. Norfolk Botanical Garden has an Eagle Cam,[1] a great way to watch bald eagles building nests, caring for their young, hunting, and hanging out—all without kidnapping or terrifying the birds.

2. **Turn the channel when Jack Hanna or some other Hollywood animal wrangler comes on the air.** These folks imprison and exploit animals for their own profit. Don't be fooled by slick marketing.

3. **Enjoy only those circuses and other shows that use willing human performers.**

4. **Research before you go to the movies.** Despite phenomenal advances in computer-generated imagery (CGI), some films still use live animals. Don't go see those. Instead, go see movies that take advantage of technology to tell great stories.

---

1. See http://norfolkbotanicalgarden.org/eagles/eagle-cam-videos/.

A Shorter List of Don'ts:

1. Don't go to a circus that uses animals. Just don't. Also avoid roadside, petting, and city zoos; aquariums; carriage horse, camel, or other novelty animal rides; and diving mule shows. I manage to have a lot of fun with my kid without resorting to paying people who are cruel to animals, and you probably can, too.

2. Don't buy from advertisers that use live animals in commercials, and email or tweet at them to tell them why.

3. Basically, if a place is forcing animals to live in a pathetic approximation of their natural environment and/or forcing them to do tricks and making a profit off of them, don't give them your money.

— 21 —

Your Animal Companions

WHEN MY HUSBAND AND I go out of town, we leave a document of instructions for whatever brave soul has agreed to house/dog/cat sit for us while we're away. The document, called "Animal House" as a tribute to my hometown of Eugene, Oregon, has evolved over the years. Early iterations of the document from our first years as a married couple, when our brood was a great deal younger, range up to four pages of single-spaced instructions. Overkill? Maybe. But when you adopt a couple of high-anxiety dogs, one of whom doesn't get along with your old lady cats, you take precautions.

I didn't always give my companion animals the consideration they deserved. I have a vivid memory from my middle school years of yanking my dog Coconut down our street on her red leash attached to a choke chain, irritated that she wanted to stop and sniff so many things. She was a fifteen-pound cock-a-poo and I manhandled her. When we had a puppy, Lucy, who wouldn't stop chewing the laundry, we gave her away. She was poisoned a short time later by neighbors of the family we gave her to. We bought dogs from backyard breeders. We once bought a purebred kitten, Walter, the sweetest little man, who died six months later of feline immunodeficiency virus. We had to euthanize Heidi, a purebred lab in her prime, because of a horrible skin disorder. When our animals relieved themselves on the floor, we pushed their faces in it and we swatted them with newspapers.

We weren't bad people. And we weren't mercilessly abusive. Our dogs and cats lived inside with us, slept in our beds and on the couches, got regular vet visits and lots of love and playtime. And my parents readily extended this love to strays, as well. When we saw animals running down the street, my dad would cajole them into our garage, we'd make some inquiring calls, and then take them to the shelter, where they had the best chance at being reunited with their humans. Sometimes, my dad would check up on them. I remember one shepherd mix, Jack, whose picture showed up in the "Pet of the Week" (read: last chance before the needle) section of the newspaper. My dad was bummed at the thought that Jack might have to be put down. Ten years after she passed, I flipped the visor of my dad's truck down one sunny day and a photo of Heidi on her last day fluttered into my lap. Coconut and Walter were lovingly buried in our side yard so we could visit with them while we mourned. When Simon, the baby chick from my high school biology class, injured his leg, my mother let him sleep curled up on her collarbone, nestled in her long hair. My parents and I may have made a few mistakes along the way, but they taught me to love species other than my own.

Having learned some lessons over the years (and gained some wisdom, I hope), I have drawn up a list of dos and don'ts to help guide you in your day-to-day life with the animals in your care. But more than I want to guide you, I want to encourage you to love. You probably don't share your home with a lion or a gorilla, animals who could tear you limb from limb if they wanted to. If you're like a lot of Americans, you may have a dog or cat, guinea pig, rabbits or birds. It's pretty likely your companion animals rely on you for food, shelter, and care. It's pretty likely that you have more physical power than your animal companions and that they are constantly at your mercy. This is just a sliver, a murky reflection, of the power of God in our lives, and God chooses to deal with us mercifully. God sacrifices for us—paid the ultimate sacrifice for us.

As I write this, the humans in my house are outnumbered by the nonhumans. Among the mix are two dogs, Clyde and Bradley. Bradley is a hound puppy, just a year old, with all the energy and precociousness of a toddler. Clyde is nearing a decade of life. An eighty-pound, high-strung lug who had been taken into and then thrown out of five or six homes before he was six months old. He's food obsessed and will put his giant paws on the kitchen counter to grab any food in sight the moment your back is turned. If you're in *his* chair or *his* spot, he'll just stand and stare at you until you move. He drives me crazy, and yet when I think of the immanent possibility of life without him, I am reminded to treat him more gently, use a kinder tone of voice, and forgive his doggy mistakes. I think God does that with us, too.

And now the list, for those who like that sort of thing:

1. Always adopt, never buy, companion animals. Shelters are overrun with dogs and cats, but you can also find rabbits, birds, and other small animals at shelters and rescue organizations around the globe.

2. Before you adopt, consider your motivations. Is your desire to have an animal in your home an outpouring of love or are you hoping to use the animal for some purpose—as a cheap alarm system, for example? If it's the latter, perhaps finding a nonsentient way to manage would be better for both you and your potential housemate.

3. Spay and neuter your animals and, if you can afford to, spay and neuter your friends' and family's animals, too. There are cheap clinics run by dedicated folks all over the nation who will help you do this.

4. Humans might choose to have their bodies mutilated, but let's not do that to our companions. Declawing, tail and ear docking, and wing clipping are painful and unnecessary mutilations.

5. Clean the litter box at least twice a day. You don't like going in dirty toilets, and neither do cats.

6. Keep cats inside, unless you can supervise them outside (via cat fences or on leashes . . . yes, leashes, it's not impossible).

7. Provide regular veterinary care. Know the location and phone number of the nearest emergency veterinary clinic.

8. Let dogs out (or walk them) frequently. Imagine how boring and painful it would be to have to hold your bladder for eight or ten or twelve hours straight.

9. Your dog's walks are for your dog, not you. Plan to go at a leisurely pace. Let her sniff—this is her time to explore the world.

10. Dogs should never be kept outside in pens or on a chain. Chained and penned dogs become aggressive and fearful.

11. Please don't crate your dog, unless it's for short periods in the car or to keep them safe while repair people are coming and going. Can you imagine spending all day in a box? If your dogs, like mine, create havoc when you leave your home, choose a decent-sized room in which they can't do a lot of damage and have a view of the world outside, provide loads of toys and bedding, and remember that being a good person is a lot more important than having perfect furnishings.

12. Collar 101 for Dogs: harnesses and breakaway collars = yes! Electric, prong, and choke collars = no.

13. Collar 101 for Cats: breakaway = yes! Flea = no. Flea collars have been known to burn cats' skin. There are far safer ways to prevent infestation.

14. Dogs and cats are a ten-to-twenty-year commitment. If you can't make that commitment, through moves and marriages and babies and midlife crises, don't. And if you do find that you *must* get rid of Fifi or Fido, have the guts and compassion to take them to your veterinarian and hold and comfort them while your vet performs the euthanasia. Animals attach themselves to us. We are their pack and their providers. We owe it to them to protect them from the chaos and fear of being dumped in a shelter, passed from home to home, or winding up with an abuser. Euthanasia by injection in the leg is a fast, painless, and completely peaceful way to die. Don't be selfish—give your companion a good life and a good death.

15. Remember the golden rule: do unto others. I think it applies most especially to the least of these.

16. Finally, if you can't or won't do these basic things, don't get an animal. Just don't. Really. Don't. I'm serious.

22

PETA's Community Animal Project

(AND HOW YOU CAN HELP ANIMALS IN YOUR OWN COMMUNITY)

EVERY YEAR, LIKE CLOCKWORK, a group of lobbying organizations that represent breeders and factory farms get together and announce the shocking news that PETA kills animals. It's a good headline, right? Your average Jane might assume that advocating for animals means keeping them alive at all costs, life for life's sake.

But sometimes, living is no life at all. That's especially true for the dogs and cats encountered by PETA's Community Animal Project (CAP) day after day, year after year. When I worked at PETA's headquarters in Norfolk, I had a couple of opportunities to go out into our surrounding community with the CAP fieldworkers. They were the hardest and most memorable days of my time in Norfolk.

Let me say right off the bat that I'm not cut out for fieldwork. I'm afraid of most strange dogs, don't like to touch dirty things, and really dislike being dirty myself. I'm an indoor kitty.

My first time in the field, I was part of a volunteer contingent from the office who joined with other animal rescue organizations in the region to remove dozens of dogs from a sprawling rural property. As we drove into the property, we passed dog after dog, mostly chocolate lab/pit bull mixes, chained to empty oil drums, tree limbs, and heavy tires. These dogs were mostly isolated from one another. It was spring and the ground was thick with mud and feces. Deeper into the property, we began to see makeshift kennels: high fences formed in circles no more than twenty feet in diameter, each containing a single doghouse or ramshackle shelter and at least half a dozen wild, scared, and filthy dogs. Many of the dogs ran from human contact; a very few were more aggressive. One by one, we caught these dogs and led or carried them (perhaps one or two had ever been on a leash before—most were simply terrified and unable to move) to waiting vans full of cages for transport to local shelters. We removed dozens of dogs. For those we had to leave behind, we threw down bale after bale of straw, until finally the mud ceased soaking through and the dogs had something firm to step on, something warm to nestle in.

My next foray into the field wasn't for several more years, when I went on a ride-along to North Carolina to see what a typical day was like for my colleagues in CAP. It was sweltering. I don't remember the season.

We started the day with a couple of brief stops. At the first house, a new manufactured home, we checked in on two dogs who were kept tied to trees in the side yard. One dog had become badly tangled in her worn cable-wire chain and there were deep, raw cuts on her legs. We treated her wounds, replaced her tie-out, gave her and her companion toys, left instructions for her people, and moved on. Here, as in many other cases, the dogs "belonged" to a relative or friend of the homeowner, who didn't have the means, time, or will to care for the creatures left on their property. At our second stop, we checked on two Great Dane puppies whose person was an elderly man who kept these big, energetic dogs in a small gated kennel. We let the pups out, let them jump on us and gave them love before leaving. At another home, we checked on a tiny puppy, Diamond, who had been collared and chained to a crate at the side of a house with no food, water, or shelter in sight. My colleague documented the dog's condition and wrote a report to submit to the local authorities, but her hopes were not high that they would take action.

In addition to the scheduled stops—the pups whom CAP regularly checks on to monitor their situation and develop a relationship with their owners—fieldworkers inevitably stumble on cases of serious neglect. This day was no exception. We pulled over once to ensure that a dog lying on the side of the highway was fully dead. She was, along with the babies she had been carrying. We stopped at a beautiful home along a wide road when we spotted a lone dog chained to a tree, more than one hundred feet behind the house, with nothing but an old blue barrel to use as shelter. This shepherd mix puppy was energetic and incredibly friendly but wasn't allowed to go into the house, and it was clear that he had been mostly forgotten, consigned to life alone in a ten-foot circle of the backyard. At another home, we saw another filthy (and huge) dog trapped in a tiny pen with no shelter, food, or water.

We climbed high into the hills for one of our scheduled stops and were "greeted" by two scared, snarling dogs so badly infected with mange that there was no fur left on them. Their owner, a woman who lived in a trailer with no electricity or plumbing, cried as she signed them over for euthanasia. She was unable to afford veterinary care, food, or shelter for the dogs, who were suffering terribly as a result. The dogs were terrified of her, and of us, but we were able to use wet dog food to calm them down so that they would allow us to approach them and get them into the van. At our final stop, a Doberman was surrendered to us. It was obvious that he had never known human companionship. He was terrified, and for the three-hour drive back to PETA's headquarters, he lay quietly on the floor of the van, his face buried in my lap, periodically urinating in fear.

My Doberman friend was the first dog I have seen euthanized. I held him as the needle was inserted into his foreleg and lowered him gently to the ground as he lost consciousness. He was gone in the blink of an eye, released from a world that had shown him no kindness. After a hearty meal and much love, the two mange-ridden dogs followed.

This day, these dogs, represent just a tiny fraction of the evil faced by nonhuman companion animals at the mercy of self-absorbed, cruel, or unwitting humans. Each day, in shelters across the nation, thousands of animals are surrendered, a myriad of excuses given. I pulled these statistics from the Oxford-Lafayette Humane Society in Mississippi:

- Number of cats and dogs born every day in the U.S.: seventy thousand (nearly three thousand born every hour, or fifty every minute)

- Number of stray cats and dogs living in the U.S.: seventy million

- Number of animals in the U.S. who die each year from cruelty, neglect, and exploitation: thirty million

- Number of animal shelters in the U.S.: four thousand to six thousand

- Number of cats and dogs entering U.S. shelters each year: six to eight million

- Number of cats and dogs euthanized by U.S. shelters each year: three to four million (nearly ten thousand animals killed every day)

- Number of cats and dogs adopted by U.S. shelters each year: three to four million

- Number of cats and dogs reclaimed by owners from U. S. shelters each year: 600,000 to 750,000 (10 percent of total entering shelters—15 to 30 percent of dogs and 2 to 5 percent of cats)

- Yearly cost to U.S. taxpayers to impound, shelter, euthanize, and dispose of homeless animals: $2 billion

- Percentage of dogs in U.S. shelters who are purebred: 25 to 30 percent

- Average age of animals entering U.S. shelters: under eighteen months old

- Percentage of animals entering U.S. shelters who are healthy and adoptable: 90 percent

- Percentage of owned dogs who were adopted from an animal shelter: 18 percent

- Percentage of owned cats who were adopted from an animal shelter: 16 percent

- Percentage of animals entering animal shelters by animal control authorities: 42.5 percent

- Percentage of animals entering animal shelters who were surrendered by their owners: 30 percent

- Percentage of people who acquire animals and end up giving them away, abandoning them, or taking them to shelters: 70 percent

- Percentage of animals surrendered to an animal shelter who were originally adopted from an animal shelter: 20 percent

- Percentage of animals received by animal shelters who have been spayed or neutered: 10 percent

You can see we have a big problem. And these are the animals we claim are our best friends!

You don't have to live next door to the world's largest animal rights organization in order to make a difference in your community. You already know how to do right by the animals in your life (see chapter 21), but there are ways to impact those animal companions who aren't lucky enough to call you mom or dad.

First, like they say at the airport: if you see something, say something. Speak up when you see cruelty or neglect and report it to the authorities. If they don't respond, hound them until they do.

Maybe your neighbors don't realize that chained dogs become aggressive and dangerous, not to mention miserable. Let them know the risks. And look into your local ordinances. If there isn't a ban on continuous chaining, get one! And if there is, make sure your local authorities are enforcing it.

Find out who offers low- or no-cost spay and neutering in your community and spread the word to family, friends, neighbors—pretty much everyone.

When someone you know says they are looking into getting a cat or dog, be sure they know how big a commitment it is and that there's no excuse for buying a dog or cat instead of rescuing from a shelter or adopting from a reputable rescue organization. For real, there's no such thing as a "hypoallergenic dog" and there are loads of breed-specific rescues.

If you do become *that person* about dogs and cats, consider extending your compassion and passion to other furry, finned, and feathered creatures, as well.

For more information on PETA's work in Virginia and North Carolina, check out their website (http://www.peta.org/about-peta/learn-about-peta/helping-animals-in-hampton-roads/community-animal-project/), and to learn how you can get active for animals in your community, visit http://www.peta.org/about-peta/learn-about-peta/helping-animals-in-hampton-roads/resources-hampton-roads/.

23

Buying Cruelty Free

IF YOU HAD TOLD me when I started buying hair spray and mascara as a teenager that it was likely that the products I was getting from the drugstore had been tested on animals, I would have freaked out in a way only pubescent girls can. Yet for some reason, it never occurred to me that my leather shoes came from a once living and breathing cow.

At some point on the journey to making more compassionate life choices, including the cessation of ratting my bangs, perming my hair, and pegging my pleated jeans, I started to buy cruelty-free products and I stopped wearing products that contained animal bits, like wool, leather, and silk.

Many people I talk to now are surprised to learn that personal care and household cleaning products are still tested on animals. Others don't realize that buying leather, fur, and wool supports cruelty to animals. Happily, if you have a computer and/or the ability to read and you're willing to cut cruelty out of your shopping list, it's pretty easy.

You can start here for lists and lists of cruelty-free companies: http://lmgtfy.com/?q=Cruelty+Free+Companies. Then, there are loads of great vegan lifestyle blogs and resources here: http://lmgtfy.com/?q=Vegan+Lifestyle+Blog. Vegans are all over Pinterest: http://www.pinterest.com/search/?q=vegan. And there are more than a hundred thousand pages indexed on Google that will ease your transition to a vegan lifestyle: http://bit.ly/1iB4yc4.

If that's information overload, here's a quick glimpse into my house . . .

In the Kitchen

- Method dish detergent and hand soap
- Seventh Generation disinfecting multi-surface cleaner
- J. R. Watkins tub and tile cleaner
- Dr. Bronner's castile soap

In the Bathroom

- JASON toothpaste
- ShiKai shampoo and conditioner
- Alba Botanica facial wash
- Kiss My Face olive and chamomile bar soap
- Kiss My Face deodorant (I like the roll-on, my husband uses a stick)
- Method tub and tile cleaner

In My Purse

- The Body Shop Hemp Hand Protector
- Alba Botanica natural Hawaiian lip balm in coconut cream—the best best best best lip balm I have ever used
- Unfortunately, after I bought a mineral powder by Mary Kay, the company started testing on animals after a couple of decades of being cruelty-free. So, it's still in my bag, but I won't buy it again until they stop that stupidity.

In My Closet

- Two incredibly warm coats, one by Beyond Fleece and the other by Anne Klein. The Anne Klein coat looks a little like shearling, so I wear anti-fur buttons on it, to be sure folks know I'm not wearing the skin of lambs.
- Totes winter boots

- Shoes from Naturalizer, the Sak, Sanuk, Merrell, Sanita (Dansko's vegan line), and Skechers

- There are also clothes in my closet, of course, but it's not that complicated to avoid animal products in clothing. Here's a nice little blog post on how to start shopping a little differently for clothes: http://mllevegan.com/2014/01/17/veganize-your-wardrobe/.

When I decided to stop using animal products and products tested on animals, I took a conservative approach. I used up or wore out the things I had that no longer jived with my ethical view and replaced them with things that did. There's a saying that I like: progress, not perfection. Making little choices at the drugstore checkout line may not seem earth-changing, but add your actions to the many who have gone before and will come after, all around the world . . . and eventually, we'll see a shift in how folks conceive of their relationships with animals. Progress, not perfection.

24

Public Policies

I'M GOING TO OFFER this chapter with a caveat.

Public policies that give nonhuman animals some relief from miserable lives of torment are important. When a law is passed and enforced, it may help many animals.

Do you sense a "but" coming?

Here it is: But the first thing we *must* do is look at the suffering we cause by the choices we make in our everyday lives. Accusations leveled at an owner who chains his dog outside twenty-four hours a day ring hollow when they're spewed from the mouth of one who eats the flesh of animals who have suffered in similar ways. I'll say it again: progress, not perfection, but the danger is that we will love and protect the ones who are easy to love and protect—the ones we call companions—and stop there. We draw arbitrary lines between species (a classification that is itself fairly arbitrary) and then enact or withhold justice and mercy based on those constructs.

Secondly, while I'm in favor of laws that protect animals, we know that "love is the fulfilling of the law." Forced change is often necessary, but it's sustainable when those changes come out of heart transformation. We can't force people by law to be good. Transformation and reconciliation are Holy Spirit works. Our responsibility is to be faithful to the leading of that Spirit, and to love.

Some Basics

There are two major federal laws that govern the treatment of nonhuman animals: the Animal Welfare Act (AWA) and the Humane Methods of Livestock Slaughter Act (or Humane Slaughter Act, HSA).

The AWA, passed in 1966, applies to those who traffic in nonhuman animals (as pets or entertainment, for instance) and governs the use of nonhuman animals in laboratories. The AWA sets out some very minimum standards of care. One major problem with the act, however, is that it only covers warm-blooded species and specifically excludes birds, rats, and mice. We don't know exactly how many mice and rats are used in laboratories because they are given no more consideration than test tubes or petri dishes, despite their sentience. As a result, only about 5 percent of animals used in laboratories are actually covered by the AWA. So, that's a win (#not).

The HSA is pretty much what it sounds like: a law designed to ensure that animals are rendered insensible to pain prior to having their throats slit open and their skin and limbs hacked off. The law was passed in 1958, as factory farming was beginning to take hold in the U.S., but long before it was the status quo. The USDA has recorded slaughter counts as far back as 1907 for cows pigs, and sheep. They didn't start to track bird slaughter until 1960, and since then the number of chickens slaughtered per month in the U.S. has increased sevenfold, from 105 million in January 1960 to more than 700 million in January 2014. The percentages of chickens and turkeys slaughtered have also increased dramatically, from just under 85 percent of the total number of animals in January 1960 to nearly 97 percent of the total in January 2014.[1]

Here's the super fun part: *birds (chickens and turkeys) are specifically excluded from protection under the HSA*. Do you get the significance of that? Nearly 97 percent of the animals we kill for food in the United States aren't covered by the *one* law that protects animals in slaughterhouses. The Animal Welfare Institute points out that "although the US Congress has never repealed the humane slaughter laws of 1958 and 1978, the laws are blatantly disregarded. The large-scale plants move animals so rapidly through the slaughter lines that it is impossible to stun and kill them humanely. Animals

---

1. You, too, can look at giant spreadsheets of historical slaughter figures and do your own depressing analysis because the Economic Research Service of the United States Department of Agriculture is at your disposal. I wonder what would happen if the USDA spent more time, I don't know, *protecting* animals and less time updating Excel documents?

may be dismembered or scalded while still alive and conscious, their cries echoing through the plants. Succumbing to industry pressure, the USDA is failing to enforce the law as mandated by the US Congress."[2]

To be perfectly clear, the HSA only protects animals *at* the slaughter-house, where they spend a fraction of their miserable lives. There are no federal laws that protect animals on factory farms or during transport *to* the slaughterhouse.

So, to sum up: the only federal law in the United States that protects animals in laboratories specifically excludes about 95 percent of animals used in labs, and the only federal law in the United States that protects animals used for food specifically excludes about 97 percent of animals slaughtered and protects the rest only in the last few hours of their horrible lives.

Localized Legislative Efforts

State by state, activists on both sides of the animal welfare fight are working to enact legislation. This isn't meant to be an exhaustive list of all animal (or anti-animal) protection efforts, just a primer. Perhaps some of these are topics on the table in your region. In that case, this review can give you some points to consider as you weigh whether or not to support any given proposal.

As with all legislative efforts, it's important to get beyond the rhetoric and sound bites and figure out who's really behind any given legislation. Who stands to gain from a law being passed or defeated? Who wrote the law, and what prompted them to do so? Many detractors call into question the motives behind animal protection legislation, but I'd ask, what does an animal activist group really stand to gain by pouring time, resources, and energy into, say, a veal crate ban? Accolades and perhaps a small, temporary uptick in donations? But those who would work against such a ban—are they simply out to protect their bottom line? And when it comes to passing legislation, which should be given more weight: profit margin or pain?

I believe that Christians are specially called to speak healing, whole-ness, and reconciliation into our public spheres, and we must carefully con-sider the values we proclaim when we make even the smallest of decisions.

2. Animal Welfare Institute, "Humane Methods of Slaughter," par. 3. The AWI has some good basic primers on legislation pertaining to animals on its site (https://awion-line.org/).

Do we claim justice and mercy? How do we live into the awesome privilege of the *imago Dei*?

There is an insidious legislative effort now making state-by-state appearances. "Ag gag" laws make it a crime to gain employment at a farm or slaughterhouse under false pretenses and criminalize the activities typically associated with undercover investigations. Ag gag laws are the epitome of shooting the messenger. Instead of protecting animals from harm and urging more transparency in agricultural practice and procedure, ag gag laws protect abusers from exposure and ensure that the kinds of atrocities discussed in chapter 18 go unreported and uncorrected. If an ag gag law comes up in your state, I'd urge you to prayerfully consider joining with local advocates to quash the effort. Ag gag laws are really no good, no good at all.

There are, however, some legislative efforts that might be worth supporting. Here is a quick rundown of a few recent types of animal protection legislation:

- **Gestation and veal crate bans:** These are both tiny spaces in which animals are confined for long periods of time in order to limit their movement. Getting rid of them is a good thing. *If* we are going to use nonhuman animals for human gain (and by now perhaps you also believe that animals are not ours to use), we are absolutely responsible for providing care and consideration for their God-given needs, including the need to nurture and be nurtured by others of the same species. Baby cows should be with their mothers, and mother pigs should have the freedom to walk about, turn around, and lie down in comfort. I don't know about you, but if I'd had to spend my pregnancy in a crate, I would have wanted to die.

- **Increased cage size for chickens:** They would get the equivalent of a legal-sized sheet of paper, instead of a letter-sized sheet! Many animal advocates rail against this kind of barely registered incremental change, fearing that it doesn't actually improve living conditions for animals and might act as a salve for the conscious of those who profit off of or consume animal products. I admit that the argument is compelling and I haven't yet come to a definitive conclusion on the best strategy. So, for the time being, until I hear a word from the Lord, I want to decrease suffering where possible, and a tiny bit more room is better than no more room.

- **Puppy mill bans:** You'd think these would be a piece of cake, because everyone loves puppies, but it turns out that animal breeders are hugely invested in keeping the government out of their backyards. I personally would prefer a ban on the sale of any animal, whether they were bred and born in a puppy mill or the Ritz-Carlton. There are far too many homeless dogs to continue the sham of breeding and buying. "Every time someone buys, a shelter dog dies." Remember that mantra. Have it tattooed somewhere.

- **Chaining ordinances:** If your dogs are like mine, they greet you as if you're the prodigal daughter every single day after work. Sure, they're home with someone almost all day, but when a new person walks in the door . . . schoowee, it's like Christmas. Dogs are wired to be part of a pack, to have a leader, to have a job, to have companions. So in addition to being just downright mean, chaining dogs is a public health hazard because, like people who live in isolation, dogs who aren't afforded basic companionship are likely to lash out.

- **Cruelty-to-animals statutes and increased penalties:** The consequences for cruelty to animals vary wildly from state to state. You might get a slap on the wrist for intentionally starving or burning your dog in one state, while it's a felony in another. Here's the truth, though: people who abuse animals rarely stop there. Animal abuse is a proven warning sign for escalated violence against humans. So *even if* you don't value the lives of nonhuman animals (but, really, I hope by now you do), concern for our own safety and well-being should compel us to ensure that animal abusers receive the help they need and are prevented from causing further harm.

- **Bullhook bans:** Yes, I think it's a good idea to ban the use of an instrument whose sole purpose is to beat elephants into submission.

- **Restrictions on the ownership of exotic animals:** The earth is the Lord's and everything in it. We don't own animals; we're charged with their care. And it's unlikely that a petting zoo or circus is going to bend over backwards to ensure that lions, tigers, and bears are provided the space and enrichment they require for full, healthy lives. There are some legitimate sanctuaries that rescue exotic animals from zoos or the film industry and that do a good job of caring for those animals. We should support them. But if Uncle Larry wants to get a capuchin monkey because Paris Hilton did once, we should suggest he find a different use of his time and money.

- **Bans on cockfighting, dogfighting, and dog racing:** Yes, please.

- **Getting great apes out of laboratories:** Great apes are condemned to lives of misery because they share so much of our human DNA. "They are like us, intelligent and capable of innovation and communication. Let's keep them in cages for many decades and see what they do when we deprive them of contact, see what happens when we bash their heads into concrete, when we give them diseases. They are like us, so we can learn much from them." Wait, what? I hope by now you are convinced that "like" and "unlike" are not adequate categories when it comes to determining how much one may or may not disregard the needs and worth of another created being. I want all animals out of labs, yes, but getting great apes out would be a good first step toward acknowledging that vivisection is neither morally nor scientifically justifiable.

Conclusion

As I said, this isn't an exhaustive list of legislative possibilities. We didn't talk about the Endangered Species Act, exceptions to antiwhaling laws for indigenous tribes, bans on the import of certain animal products (like ivory or seal fur), poaching and hunting laws, or issues outside of the United States. If you want to learn more about legal protections for animals, or ways to advocate for nonhuman animals in the legal sphere, the Animal Legal Defense Fund is a great resource. You can find them online at aldf.org.

$$--- 25 ---$$

Frequently Asked Questions

THESE ARE JUST A smattering of the most common questions I have been asked by friends and family since becoming an "animal person." If you have your own, or want a more thorough answer, or want to dialogue or protest, feel free to drop me a line at sarahwithrowking.com. I'd love to hear from you.

If you've decided to make a change in your life, you may get some of these questions as well. You might be feeling particularly convicted by the Holy Spirit and the questions may start to irritate you. Your instinct might be to want to shout from the rooftops, to point at every fur-wearer at Christmas Eve service and holler, "*J'accuse!*" But if you want to help open people's hearts to the suffering that you now experience, it's important to keep a few things in mind:

1. Always be kind. There's a place for anger, but not for self-righteousness. Someone gently opened your eyes to these issues; you now have the opportunity to do the same.

2. Dinner is a terrible time to go into graphic detail about cruelty to animals. If you give a gory speech every time someone asks a question, you'll stop getting invitations and, therefore, opportunities. Instead of describing cruelty in vivid detail, briefly explain the ethic behind your decision and offer to send or give your dinner companion more information. I once emailed a gal a list of videos to watch after we talked over lunch. They sat in her inbox for a year before she got up the courage to watch them, but watch them she did—and made changes as a result.

3. Remember that the timing isn't in your hands. This is truly a God thing.

4. When your conversation partners get defensive or lash out, let their reactions roll off your back. Remember that it's hard for folks to hear things that may require them to make a change and that you were in their shoes once. Answer questions with humility and grace.

So, here are some of the most frequently asked questions and my responses to them. I don't always take my own advice. I guess I'm human like that.

Where do you get your protein?

Protein isn't a nutrient specific to animal-based foods. There's protein in pretty much everything I consume, from spinach to lentils to vegan ice cream. A lot of folks in the United States actually consume too much protein, so really, if you're reading this book, it's highly unlikely you are risking a protein deficiency by switching from steak to soy.

That said, I'm not a vegan for health reasons and have found that a lot of folks who stop eating animals for their own health eventually go back to eating them for one reason or another. There's science and pseudoscience on both sides of the animal protein debate. I don't really care. My family and I are healthy on a plant-based, mostly whole-food diet. Not everyone can do that. Some people have crazy allergies or are severely anemic. If you really want to stop animal suffering but for some reason fourteen doctors have told you that you must eat animal protein, I don't think you are a disappointment to God and I hope you don't think that, either. Maybe the best you can do in this life is to get to know and buy from your local farmer who, at the very least, does the best she can do to care for and kill the animals you buy. And maybe donate a little of the money God provides you to an organization that works to raise awareness of animal suffering or the environmental devastation wrought by factory farming.

Romans 14:3 says, "Those who eat must not despise those who abstain, and those who abstain must not pass judgment on those who eat; for God has welcomed them." In other words, what we choose to eat or to avoid must not cause divisions in the church. God welcomes all who want to draw closer to their Creator, to be in Christian community, and to follow Jesus. Do I think humans, the world, and animals are better off when humans aren't eating other created animals? Yes. But if you disagree, let's still both go to the Sunday potluck, and invite some friends.

How did you give up [fill in animal food of choice]?

I just did. I fought cravings for months, and still do sometimes. But the thought of eating animals no longer brings me joy. Watch enough slaughterhouse and undercover investigation footage and you'll soon feel the same.

Don't cows have to be milked?

Not by humans, no. Cows are mammals who produce milk after giving birth to a baby cow. At some point, humans thought they'd try drinking cow's milk. I don't know, maybe they tried horse or dog milk first but found it unsatisfying. Me, I would have thought to steer clear of a food that helped make baby cows into one-ton bulls but that's another story.

Now we have a worldwide industry dedicated to impregnating cows, taking their babies away and turning them into veal or another pregnant cow, taking their milk, impregnating them again, taking their babies away again, taking their milk, etc. Humans are the only species to drink milk after infancy, and the only species to drink the milk of another species. We don't do that because we are made in the image of God; we do that because we've developed a taste and habit for cow's milk. And tastes can be as easily un-developed as developed. There are loads of cow's milk alternatives, and for the eco- and cost-conscious, it's pretty easy to make your own soy, rice, or almond milk at home.

What's wrong with eggs?

See chapter 11 for information on how chickens are raised and killed for their flesh and eggs. There are folks out there who *totally* do right by their chickens—keep a small number, don't kill them for their flesh, and gather and eat their eggs. Fine. That's fine. But if you're not besties with one of those folks, the chickens who laid your eggs led a miserable life and will have a terrifying death.

Is peanut butter vegan?

My dear friend Bill actually asked me this once. Someone else asked about cocoa butter. Answer: yes, to both. And I love you, Bill.

Don't you miss [fill in animal food of choice]?

Yes. Frequently. But just because I miss something or it gives me fleeting satisfaction doesn't mean I can or should pursue that thing. I'm not saying we all need to be ascetics—Jesus knew how to party (water into wine, yo!), but Jesus also inaugurated the reign of God on earth. In other words, we need to enjoy our time on earth responsibly. We aren't hanging out here, hoping for the world to disintegrate so that we can all be swept up into a fluffy heaven where the streets are paved with conflict-free gold. Jesus taught us to pray, "Thy kingdom *come.*" Thy kingdom come. Come to us, come here. As we live in the tension of an "already, but not yet" reign of God, we don't throw our hands up in despair or wring them in fright; we get in there, get dirty, and make the hard decisions that reflect what ought to be instead of settling for what is.

What about humane/cage-free/all-natural/grass-fed [animal]?

There's a difference between marketing and actual, regulated rules. "Organic" is a regulated term and provides some very, *very* basic rules for animal care. All of the phrases in the question are marketing terms and totally meaningless. Let me say that again. Phrases like "humane" and "grass-fed" are absolutely, totally, utterly meaningless. They are phrases used to get guilty rich people to spend more money. "Cage-free" on a carton of eggs just means that the hens who laid those eggs were on the floor of a giant warehouse. *Maybe* there was a small hole through which a few dozen of the thousands of chickens could sometimes squeeze into the outside air, but not necessarily. If you don't visit a place to see firsthand how animals there are raised and killed, you simply cannot know from the packaging what an animal's life and death was like. Further, even an "organic" label doesn't change the fact that all animals raised and killed for food meet the same painful, terrifying fate at the slaughterhouse.

What do you eat?!

I eat a lot of food. I love food. And I've been able to eat healthy vegan food all across the United States, from Pensacola to Eugene, Norfolk to Philadelphia. There's soymilk at coffee shops in Missoula, vegan barbeque in Boise, and delicious vegan milkshakes in Chicago. Search online for "vegetarian starter kit" or "vegan transition" or something along those lines and you will find loads of step-by-step guides and information to help you make a change. When I went vegan, I bought a couple of vegan cookbooks and just started to buy different food. And I ate out less. It was cheaper, healthier, and easier than I ever thought.

Isn't it okay to use animal products, as long as the animals are treated well?

I'm giving this a highly qualified "yes." My reading of scripture doesn't disallow humans to steward and partner with nonhuman creation in a mutually beneficial way. Some animals like having a "job" (my dogs are particularly proud of their ability to loudly and persistently let us know when a cat trespasses into our backyard), and it's fine to provide food, shelter, veterinary care, and affection to an animal who does a little work around the house for you. Hebrew law demanded a regular Sabbath and extended that rest to nonhuman animals. But let's not fool ourselves—folks who ask this question aren't typically wondering if it's okay for them to use a horse to plow their field; they're wondering if they can feel okay about eating steak because the menu says that the cow was "grass-fed" and "humanely raised." Or they really want to take a carriage ride but aren't sure of the ethics of using horses to pull lazy tourists through congested city streets on ninety-five-degree days. So, sure, if our intentions are to steward, protect, and provide for nonhuman animals and their labor produces something without coercion or suffering, fine, use that. But let's be clever, not simple, in our discerning (Prov 14:15).

Isn't eating meat the natural thing to do? We've done it for so long . . .

We enslaved people for a long time, too, and thought that it was natural and true that people with dark skin were born to serve people with light skin. We thought it was okay to make children work in mines and factories because they were our property. We thought women didn't really have the mental or physical acumen to think through the voting process. We were wrong. It's pretty easy to see where previous generations really messed up, but a little harder to look around at what's happening today and wonder where we might be perpetuating suffering. "That's just the way we've always done it" is as bad in ethics and Christian practice as it is in business.

But farms existed in biblical times, just as they exist now. If they were so bad, wouldn't the Bible have said something?

Farming in first-century Palestine or ancient Israel looked nothing like today's factory farms, which didn't come into existence until the mid-twentieth century. If the whole world consumed flesh only from animals raised and killed on farms where the sheep and goats and chickens were truly well cared for and probably even slept inside with you, I might be in a different line of work.

Does my going vegetarian really do any good? It took more than one person opposing slavery for enslaved people to be freed.

Here's a question for you: would you rather have been the first slave owner to free enslaved people because you realized slavery was wrong, or the guy who hung on and didn't let go until the law and peer pressure forced him to give up his slaves? Another: when a teenager in your congregation is facing an unplanned pregnancy, do you give her support, encouragement, and love and let her know that her baby will be loved, or do you stand back and let her choose an abortion, since you're just one person, and it's just one baby? And another: is there something about eating vegetarian that prevents you from working against human trafficking or racism?

Jesus asked us to do audacious things, like hang out with lepers and Samaritans and be generally uncomfortable in life. Does your going vegetarian make a dent in the huge agribusiness complex? No, of course not, but why would that stop you from making a decision that you know to be right? Jesus's life and death didn't topple the Roman Empire as first-century Palestinians hoped it would, but that didn't stop him from going to the cross (and making a few waves on his way there). Here's some more encouragement:

Therefore, since we are surrounded by so great a cloud of witnesses, let us also lay aside every weight and the sin that clings so closely, and let us run with perseverance the race that is set before us, looking to Jesus the pioneer and perfecter of our faith, who for the sake of the joy that was set before him endured the cross, disregarding its shame, and has taken his seat at the right hand of the throne of God. (Heb 12:1–2)

Then the disciples came to Jesus privately and said, "Why could we not cast it out?" He said to them, "Because of your little faith. For truly I tell you, if you have faith the size of a mustard seed, you will say to this mountain, 'Move from here to there,' and it will move; and nothing will be impossible for you." (Matt 17:19–20)

For the time has come for judgment to begin with the household of God; if it begins with us, what will be the end for those who do not obey the gospel of God? . . . Therefore, let those suffering in accordance with God's will entrust themselves to a faithful Creator, while continuing to do good. (1 Pet 4:17, 19)

Shouldn't you focus on stopping abuse, instead of getting people to go cold turkey from animal products?

First, liberate your language! Then, let's do both and not get caught up in false binaries. One good way to indicate that you don't support abuse is to refuse to participate in industries that perpetuate that abuse, and to encourage your friends and family to do the same.

I got my dog from a responsible breeder/neighbor/crazy aunt. That's okay, right?

Never buy an animal from a breeder or pet store. Never. Never take a free kitten from a neighbor without first making sure that the mama cat has been spayed. Every year, between six and eight million animals are surrendered to shelters and more than half are euthanized. That's three to four million adorable, mostly adoptable, animals dead because of folks who breed and buy animals. No one knows how many more are abandoned and simply left to fend for themselves on the streets. Allergies? Go to a rescue that specializes in a specific breed. Worried about your new pet getting along with your kids? Adopt an animal who's been fostered by someone with kids.

There are *no excuses* for not rescuing or adopting an animal. None. And once you make the choice, know that you are making a ten-to-twenty-year commitment, 'til death do you part.

What about euthanasia? How can you support shelters that kill animals?

I think it's so funnynotfunny that some human animals like dominion to mean "permission to eat" when it comes to pigs, chickens, and cows but "dress in sweaters and give chemotherapy for cancer" when it comes to dogs and cats.

A dear, sweet dog who got very old and very sick was cared for by a close friend of mine. As he watched her struggle, he wrestled with the idea of whether or not it was ethical for him to make the decision to end her life. Isn't life and death in God's hands? Yes, ultimately. But remember that the stewardship and dominion we discussed in chapters 9 and 10 point to a partnership and use of power that benefits other creatures. Euthanasia, when properly administered, is a merciful end to suffering and is absolutely a proper application of our healthy stewardship of nonhuman creation. When it comes to open-admission shelters that euthanize healthy animals due to lack of space and lack of good homes, I say a prayer for those workers who, day after day, must listen to the ridiculous reasons people give for surrendering their animals, and those who, day after day, wield a needle and watch life after life slip away because of human selfishness. PETA has written extensively on the myth of the no-kill shelter, the terrible reality of warehousing animals, and the need to pursue a no-birth nation via spay and neuter programs, licensing requirements, breeder fees, and other ways to bring the dog and cat overpopulation crisis under control. Check out HelpingAnimals.com for more info.

Do you go to the zoo?

No. I haven't been to every zoo in the world and I'm sure that a very few actually do an okay job of providing enrichment for animals and educating their communities about wildlife issues. But wild animals don't belong behind bars and shouldn't be bred for profit. When humans relegate non-human animals to a cage, we stunt their God-given desires and strengths.

Zoos and circuses are basically just one of the ways we humans give God a big middle finger and say, "We think we can do this better than you."

On the other hand, studying animals in the wild (à la Jane Goodall) gives us insight into animals' behaviors, emotions, and lives independent of human interference or domination. Such insights can help us better empathize with nonhuman creation and learn how to engage the extrahuman world with care and compassion rather than fear and control.

If animals aren't ours, how do you justify keeping pets?

My family adopts companions because there are millions of creatures in our country who have been bred, abused, or abandoned and who need loving homes in which to live out the remainder of their lives. I don't consider our dogs and cats to be feeling-less property. They enrich our lives and we enrich theirs. When they are in pain or suffering, we suffer. When they experience joy, we experience joy. And when the time comes to end their suffering, we do so with gentleness and dignity, and then we mourn the loss of our companion.

Epilogue

I call heaven and earth to witness against you today that I have set
before you life and death, blessings and curses. Choose life so that you
and your descendants may live . . .

—DEUTERONOMY 30:19

AN ACQUAINTANCE OF MINE who devotes her time to justice work was traveling through the Middle East one day. Stopping for lunch, she tweeted,
"Falafel, chicken, or lamb?"

I think even in life's complexities, there is one simple rule we can live
by: to choose kindness.

She chose falafel. Will you?

Glossary

animal rights. A secular way to talk about animal liberation. The idea is that, like humans who have been historically oppressed, nonhuman animals have basic rights (to be left alone, to be free from harm, etc.).

animal welfare. Animal welfare refers to the well-being of a nonhuman animal. Someone who wants to eat animals but who wants them treated in a "humane" way before they end up on a plate would be a proponent of animal welfare.

branding. For some reason, we still think it's okay to inflict third-degree burns on the skin and flesh of nonhuman animals in order to mark them as our property. We also don't give them pain relief, either before or after we subject them to this torture.

castration. Male baby pigs and cows who will not be used for breeding have their testicles cut off when they are young, as a way of reducing aggression in confined, stressful places. Sometimes, instead of using pliers or a knife, farmworkers will just wrap a rubber band around the testicles and they'll wither up and die. I don't have this particular body part, but from what I gather, most men wouldn't dig this.

commercial fishing. My family and I went fishing a couple of times when I was very young. We never caught fish. And my old boss, Ron, loves nothing more than to spend his summers on a lake in Maine, hanging in a boat and fishing all day long. It's not for me—I don't want to kill living beings for fun—but it's a hell of a lot better than commercial fishing, which is how most fish that folks eat wind up on their plates. I talk more about this in chapter 10.

creation care. This is a Jesusy way to talk about environmentalism, since we worship the Creator, not the creation. See chapter 14 for more.

cruelty-free. When a product is cruelty-free, it means it was made without harming animals. So, typically, this means that it doesn't contain any animal products and it wasn't tested on animals. It's not a regulated term, however, so every company has a different definition. It's a good idea to know who you're giving your money to. I don't think I can buy a 100 percent cotton garment made in a sweatshop in Thailand and call it "cruelty-free," whether or not it contains animal bits.

de-beak. Because the conditions in which chickens are raised are so filthy and so crowded, and because they peck one another to establish social hierarchy and dominance, farmworkers hack the nerve-ending-filled beaks off of baby chickens when they are a few days old, and again a couple of months later for hens who are used in egg production. Chickens use their beaks to sense the world. Imagine hacking your dog's nose off—it's that level of mutilation and subversion of nature we're talking about.

de-horn. Cows are also kept in cramped quarters (are you seeing the pattern here?), and to keep them from goring one another and people, their horns are cut, gouged, burned, or scooped out of their heads. Animal welfare expert Temple Grandin calls it "the single most painful thing we do"[1] to cows. And the vast majority of the time, it's done with no pain relief whatsoever.

dust-bathe. Chickens like to scratch at the earth until the dust billows, then let it settle in their feathers and shake it off. The process, called dust-bathing, helps keep their feathers and skin clean of parasites. Chickens in wire mesh cages are unable to engage in this basic, God-created hygiene practice.

factory farm. So, there's the tiny little farm your grandpa was born on and worked until he went into the army at nineteen—the farm where the family knew the names of all the pigs and the health of each individual animal really did matter. That's not how we make meat now. Like many other things, we've depersonalized and industrialized the creation of goods to purchase. So, confined animal feeding operations (CAFOs or factory farms) are the order of the day. But I want to be clear that not all small farms are run by nice people who ensure humane conditions, and certainly animals raised on

---

1. Schecter and Sandholm, "Dehorning," par. 7.

small farms are still hung upside down and slaughtered. Or, as the world's finest news source, *The Onion*, puts it, "While frail and pharmaceutical-laden factory-farm cows just droop lifelessly while awaiting their deaths, our healthy, GMO-free cattle thrash about wildly in the air, very often tearing their own delicate flesh and shattering their leg bones in a hopeless attempt to flee to the nearby 100 percent organic grassland pastures where they were free to roam during their unnaturally truncated lives."[2]

fur farm. If they're not trapped in the wild (and most are not), foxes, minks, chinchillas, rabbits, and other animals bred, raised, and killed for their fur spend their short, hellish lives on fur farms. These are basically warehouses or fields of tiny wire cages in which animals pace, spin, gnaw on their own limbs, or eat their babies because they are so insane from the stress of confinement. They aren't given veterinary care and are usually killed by anal or vaginal electrocution. If you know someone who wears fur, try to find a nice way to tell them that they are a terrible person.

gestation crate. When I was pregnant with my son, I know I longed for a concrete pad surrounded by low metal bars that would confine me to one position day in and day out. I think I would have loved eating, sleeping, and relieving myself in the same tiny space, and I know I would have liked to nurse my baby in a similar crate, but one that basically kept me lying down instead of standing up. Gosh, I wish I'd been born a mother pig. Here's how the USDA describes gestation crates: "Within the stall, the sow is unable to turn around and simple movements such as standing up or lying down may be difficult if the sow is large, because the dynamic space requirements needed to carry out these posture changes are greater than the static space requirements. Most stalls are situated within fully enclosed, climate-controlled buildings with no bedding; slatted floors allowing urine and feces to pass through into a slurry pit under the floor."[3] Sounds lovely, right? Yet the USDA's mealy-mouthed recommendations aren't to burn the gestation crates to the ground and insist that mother pigs have the benefit of at least a little straw in which to burrow. (P.S.: The USDA is terrible, unless you're judging the quality of work by how far they can bend their morals to accommodate the wishes of agribusiness. If that's how we're measuring, they're the tops!)

2. Norman, "We Raise All Our Beef Humanely," par. 6. See also "Factory-Farm-to-Table Restaurant" and "Scientists Teach Chimpanzee."

3. Marchant-Forde, "Housing and Welfare of Sows," 1.

pet overpopulation. Some of my friends refuse to bear biological children because they are concerned about human overpopulation. For dogs and cats (companion animals), the crisis of overpopulation is not potential, it's actual. Every year in the U.S. alone, between six and eight million dogs and cats are surrendered to shelters. No one knows how many more are dumped, abandoned, or given to some hapless relative or friend. About half of the animals surrendered to shelters will be euthanized because there aren't enough homes. Every time someone buys an animal from a breeder or a pet store, it's a death sentence for a homeless animal in a shelter. Always adopt, never buy, no excuses.

tail docking. Another bizarre thing we do to cows and pigs. We hack off their tails. Tails have bones and nerves and we hack them off. In what universe is this okay?

vegan. A vegan is someone who abstains from the use of any products derived from animals. Vegan items contain no animal products.

vegetarian. A vegetarian is someone who doesn't eat animal flesh. People who eat chickens and fish are not vegetarians. Please remind them of this if they try to tell you otherwise.

vivisection. *Vivus* means "alive." *Sectio* means "cutting." Yep, it's the practice of cutting up or otherwise experimenting on live animals. There are nonanimal testing methods that are more reliable than animal models, including *in vitro* testing, computer models, human simulators, and human volunteers (not in a creepy or abusive way), and we need to start using them lickety-split, please.

Bibliography

Angier, Natalie. "Pigs Prove to Be Smart, if Not Vain." *New York Times*, November 9, 2009. http://www.nytimes.com/2009/11/10/science/10angier.html?_r=2&.

Animal Welfare Institute. "Humane Methods of Slaughter Act." https://awionline.org/content/humane-methods-slaughter-act.

Aristotle. *Politics*. Translated by William Ellis. London: J. M. Dent, 1912.

Arluke, Arnold, et al. "The Relationship of Animal Abuse to Violence and Other Forms of Antisocial Behavior." *Journal of Interpersonal Violence* 14 (1999) 963–75.

Barth, Karl. *Church Dogmatics*. Edited by G. W. Bromiley and T. F. Torrance. London: T. & T. Clark, 2009.

Bauckham, Richard. *Living with Other Creatures: Green Exegesis and Theology*. Waco: Baylor University Press, 2011.

————. "Stewardship and Relationship." In *The Care of Creation: Focusing Concern and Action*, edited by R. J. Berry, 99–106. Leicester: InterVarsity, 2000.

Becker, Fiona, and Leslie French. "Making the Links: Child Abuse, Animal Cruelty and Domestic Violence." *Child Abuse Review* 13 (2004) 399–416.

Bekoff, Marc. *The Emotional Lives of Animals: A Leading Scientist Explores Animal Joy, Sorrow, and Empathy—and Why They Matter*. Novato, CA: New World Library, 2007.

Boff, Leonardo. "Leonardo Boff on the Trinity as Good News for the Poor." In *The Christian Theology Reader*, edited by Alister E. McGrath, 196–97. Malden, MA: Wiley-Blackwell, 2011.

Bonhoeffer, Dietrich. *Letters and Papers from Prison*: Enlarged ed. New York: Simon & Schuster, 1997.

Braithwaite, Victoria. *Do Fish Feel Pain?* Oxford: Oxford University Press, 2010.

Brown, Edward R. *Our Father's World: Mobilizing the Church to Care for Creation*. Downers Grove, IL: InterVarsity, 2008.

Brueggemann, Walter. *Genesis*. Atlanta: John Knox, 1982.

Bullmore, Michael A. "The Four Most Important Passages for a Christian Environmentalism." *The Trinity Journal* 19 (1998) 139–62.

Calvin, John. *Commentaries on the First Book of Moses, Called Genesis*. Vol. 1. Translated by John King. Edinburgh: Calvin Translation Society, 1847.

Camosy, Charles. *For Love of Animals: Christian Ethics, Consistent Action*. Cincinnati: Franciscan Media, 2013.

Card, Michael. "God's Own Fool." *Scandalon*. DV&A, 1986.

Carlin, George. "Pro Life, Abortion, and the Sanctity of Life." *YouTube*, August 16, 2009. https://www.youtube.com/watch?v=AvF1Q3UidWM.

Clifford, Anne M. "From Ecological Lament to a Sustainable *Oikos*." In *God's Stewards: The Role of Christians in Creation Care*, edited by Don Brandt, 247–52. Monrovia: World Vision, 2002.

Clough, David L. *On Animals*. Vol. 1, *Systematic Theology*. London: T. & T. Clark, 2012.

Crouch, Andy. "It's Time to Talk about Power." *Christianity Today*, October 2013, 35.

Cunningham, David S. "The Doctrine of the Trinity: A Thumbnail Sketch." In *Essentials of Christian Theology*, edited by William C. Placher, 76–92. Louisville: Westminster John Knox, 2007.

"Desmond Tutu on Animal Welfare: We Must Fight Injustice to Animals." *Huffington Post*, December 27, 2013. http://www.huffingtonpost.com/2013/12/27/desmond-tutu-animal-rights_n_4509188.html.

"Factory-Farm-to-Table Restaurant Proudly Serves Locally Tortured Animals." *The Onion*, November 25, 2013. http://www.theonion.com/articles/factoryfarmtotable-restaurant-proudly-serves-local,34673/.

Fang, Xiangming, and Phaedra S. Corso. "Child Maltreatment, Youth Violence, and Intimate Partner Violence." *American Journal of Preventive Medicine* 33 (2007) 281–90. http://download.journals.elsevierhealth.com/pdfs/journals/0749-3797/PIIS0749379707003492.pdf.

Fernandez, Eleazar S. *Reimagining the Human: Theological Anthropology in Response to Systemic Evil*. St. Louis: Chalice, 2004.

Fiddes, Paul S. *The Creative Suffering of God*. Oxford: Clarendon, 1988.

Fielder, Joanne, et al. "Veterinary Report: Canadian Commercial Seal Hunt, Prince Edward Island, March 2001." *International Fund for Animal Welfare*. http://www.ifaw.org/canada/node/6346.

Flynn, Clifton P. "Why Family Professionals Can No Longer Ignore Violence toward Animals." *Family Relations* 49 (2000) 87–95.

Greenpeace International. "Slaughtering the Amazon: Summary." July 2009. http://www.greenpeace.org/international/Global/international/planet-2/report/2009/7/slaughtering-the-amazon.pdf.

Greenpeace USA. "Go Vegetarian." http://www.greenpeace.org/usa/en/multimedia/goodies/green-guide/green-lifestyle/go-vegetarian/.

Griffin, Donald R. "Afterword: What Is It Like?" In *The Cognitive Animal: Empirical and Theoretical Perspectives on Animal Cognition*, edited by Marc Bekoff et al., 471–72. Cambridge: MIT Press, 2002.

Gutierrez, Karen. "Dog-Pound Killings Caught on Tape: Shootings Were Secretly Photographed." *The Cincinnati Enquirer*, August 6, 2002. http://www.enquirer.com/editions/2002/08/06/loc_dog-pound_killings.html.

Hare, Douglas R. A. *Mark*. Louisville: Westminster John Knox, 1996.

Hasel, Frank M. "Dominion." In *Eerdmans Dictionary of the Bible*, edited by David Noel Freedman, 352. Grand Rapids: Eerdmans, 2000.

Heschel, Abraham J. *The Prophets*. Vol. 1. New York: Harper, 1962.

The Humane Society of the United States. "Undercover Investigation Reveals Cruelty to Chimps at Research Lab." March 4, 2009. http://www.humanesociety.org/news/news/2009/03/undercover_investigation_chimpanzee_abuse.html.

Internal Revenue Service. "SOI Tax Stats—Individual Statistical Tables by Size of Adjusted Gross Income." http://www.irs.gov/uac/SOI-Tax-Stats---Individual-Statistical-Tables-by-Size-of-Adjusted-Gross-Income.

Jane Goodall Institute. "Chimps in Captivity: The Great Ape Protection Act Fact Sheet." http://www.janegoodall.org/chimps-GAPA-fact-sheet.

Kidwell, Clara Sue, et al. *A Native American Theology*. Maryknoll, NY: Orbis, 2001.

Kilpatrick, Kate. "Fighting Hunger in Brazil: Much Achieved, More to Do." *Oxfam International*, June 15, 2011. http://www.oxfam.org/en/grow/policy/fighting-hunger-brazil.

King, Sarah Withrow. "Peace Begins on Our Plates." *PRISM Magazine*, January/February 2013, 45. http://prismmagazine.org/peace-begins-on-our-plates/.

LaCugna, Catherine Mowry. "The Practical Trinity." *Christian Century* 109 (1992) 678–82.

Largen, Kristin Johnston. "A Christian Rationale for Vegetarianism." *Dialog: A Journal of Theology* 48 (2009) 147–57.

Lewis, C. S. *The Problem of Pain*. New York: HarperCollins, 1940.

Linzey, Andrew. *Animal Theology*. Urbana: University of Illinois Press, 1994.

———. *Christianity and the Rights of Animals*. New York: Crossroad, 1987.

———. *Why Animal Suffering Matters: Philosophy, Theology, and Practical Ethics*. Oxford: Oxford University Press, 2009.

Linzey, Andrew, and Tom Regan, eds. *Animals and Christianity: A Book of Readings*. New York: Crossroad, 1988.

Maisto, Michelle. "Eating Less Meat Is World's Best Chance for Timely Climate Change, Say Experts." *Forbes*, April 28, 2012. http://www.forbes.com/sites/michellemaisto/2012/04/28/eating-less-meat-is-worlds-best-chance-for-timely-climate-change-say-experts/.

Marchant-Forde, Jeremy N. "Housing and Welfare of Sows during Gestation." *Sow Welfare Fact Sheet*. USDA Livestock Behavior Research Unit, June 2010. http://www.ars.usda.gov/SP2UserFiles/Place/36022000/Sow%20Housing%20Fact%20Sheet.pdf.

McFague, Sallie. *The Body of God: An Ecological Theology*. Minneapolis: Fortress, 1993.

———. *Models of God: Theology for an Ecological, Nuclear Age*. Philadelphia: Fortress, 1987.

———. "Untitled Essay." In *Essentials of Christian Theology*, edited by William C. Placher, 101–15. Louisville: Westminster John Knox, 2007.

McGrath, Alister E., ed. *The Christian Theology Reader*. Malden, MA: Wiley-Blackwell, 2011.

Middleton, J. Richard. *The Liberating Image: The* imago Dei *in Genesis 1*. Grand Rapids: Brazos, 2005.

Migliore, Daniel L. *Faith Seeking Understanding: An Introduction to Christian Theology*. Grand Rapids: Eerdmans, 2004.

Miller, Daniel K. *Animal Ethics and Theology: The Lens of the Good Samaritan*. New York: Routledge, 2012.

———. "Responsible Relationship: *Imago Dei* and the Moral Distinction between Humans and Other Animals." *International Journal of Systematic Theology* 13 (2011) 323–39.

Moltmann, Jürgen. *Creating a Just Future: The Politics of Peace and the Ethics of Creation in a Threatened World*. Translated by John Bowden. London: SCM, 1989.

———. *God in Creation: A New Theology of Creation and the Spirit of God*. Translated by Margaret Kohl. Minneapolis: Fortress, 1993.

———. "God's Covenant and Our Responsibility." In *The Care of Creation: Focusing Concern and Action*, edited by R. J. Berry, 107–13. Leicester: InterVarsity, 2000.

Moritz, Joshua M. "Animals and the Image of God in the Bible and Beyond." *Dialog: A Journal of Theology* 48 (2009) 134–46.

Norman, Hank T. "We Raise All Our Beef Humanely on Open Pasture and Then We Hang Them Upside Down and Slash Their Throats." *The Onion*, January 22, 2013. http://www.theonion.com/articles/we-raise-all-our-beef-humanely-on-open-pasture-and,30983/.

Origen. "Origen on the Suffering of God." In *The Christian Theology Reader*, edited by Alister E. McGrath, 157–58. Malden, MA: Wiley-Blackwell, 2011.

PETA. "Vivisector of the Month." April 2011. http://www.peta.org/blog/vivisector-month-april-2011/.

Pimentel, David, and Marcia Pimentel. "Sustainability of Meat-Based and Plant-Based Diets and the Environment." *American Journal of Clinical Nutrition* 78 (2003) 660S–663S.

Placher, William C., ed., *Essentials of Christian Theology*. Louisville: Westminster John Knox, 2007.

Regan, Tom. "Christianity and Animal Rights: The Challenge and Promise." In *Liberating Life: Contemporary Approaches in Ecological Theology*, edited by Charles Birch et al., 73–87. Maryknoll, NY: Orbis, 1990.

Reno, R. R. *Genesis*. Grand Rapids: Brazos, 2010.

Rodriguez, Darío López. *The Liberating Mission of Jesus: The Message of the Gospel of Luke*. Translated by Stefanie E. Israel and Richard E. Waldrop. Eugene, OR: Pickwick, 2012.

Romero, Óscar. *The Violence of Love*. Compiled and translated by James R. Brockman. Maryknoll, NY: Orbis, 1988.

Schecter, Anna, and Drew Sandholm. "Dehorning: 'Standard Practice' on Dairy Farms." *ABC News*, January 28, 2010. http://abcnews.go.com/Blotter/dehorning-standard-practice-dairy-farms/story?id=9658414.

"Scientists Teach Chimpanzee to Conduct 3-Year Study on Primates." *The Onion*, August 16, 2012. http://www.theonion.com/articles/scientists-teach-chimpanzee-to-conduct-3year-study,29195/.

Sider, Ron. *Completely Pro-Life: Building a Consistent Stance on Abortion, the Family, Nuclear Weapons, the Poor*. Downers Grove, IL: InterVarsity, 1987.

———. *Just Generosity: A New Vision for Overcoming Poverty in America*. 2nd ed. Grand Rapids: Baker, 2007.

———. *Rich Christians in an Age of Hunger: A Biblical Study*. London: Hodder and Stoughton, 1977.

Silverstein, Jason. "I Don't Feel Your Pain: A Failure of Empathy Perpetuates Racial Disparities." *Slate*, June 27, 2013. http://www.slate.com/articles/health_and_science/science/2013/06/ racial_empathy_gap_people_don_t_perceive_pain_in_other_races.single.html.

Singh, Sundar. *Wisdom of the Sadhu: Teachings of Sundar Singh*. Compiled and edited by Kim Comer. Farmington, PA: Plough, 2007.

The Smithsonian Institution, National Museum of Natural History. "What Does It Mean to Be Human?" http://humanorigins.si.edu/evidence/genetics.

Spinoza, Benedict. *Ethics*. Vol. 17. In *Opera: Lateinisch und Deutch*, vol. 2, edited by Konrad Blumenstock, 526.31–528.6. Darmstadt: WissenschaftlicheBuchgesellschaft, 1980.

Stassen, Glen, and David Gushee. *Kingdom Ethics*. Downers Grove, IL: IVP Academic, 2003.

Tallichet, Suzanne E., and Christopher Hensley. "Exploring the Link between Recurrent Acts of Childhood and Adolescent Animal Cruelty and Subsequent Violent Crime." *Criminal Justice Review* 29 (2004) 304–16. http://cjr.sagepub.com/content/29/2/304. short.

Tilley, Terrence W. *The Evils of Theodicy.* Washington, DC: Georgetown University Press, 1991.

U.S. Department of Agriculture Economic Research Service. "Livestock & Meat Domestic Data." http://www.ers.usda.gov/data-products/livestock-meat-domestic-data.aspx#. UyCslFFdWxE.

———. "Pork: Supply and Disappearance (Carcass Weight, Million Pounds) and Per Capita Disappearance (Pounds)." http://www.ers.usda.gov/datafiles/Livestock_ Meat_Domestic_Data/Quarterly_red_meat_poultry_and_egg_supply_and_ disappearance_and_per_capita_disappearance/Pork/WASDE_PorkFull.pdf.

———. "Total Poultry: Supply and Disappearance (Million Pounds) and Per Capita Disappearance (Pounds)." http://www.ers.usda.gov/datafiles/Livestock_ Meat_Domestic_Data/Quarterly_red_meat_poultry_and_egg_supply_and_ disappearance_and_per_capita_disappearance/Total_poultry/WASDE_ TotalPoultryFull.pdf.

———. "U.S. Beef Industry." http://www.ers.usda.gov/topics/animal-products/cattle-beef/statistics-information.

Vidler, Alec R. "Animals." In *Windsor Sermons,* 173–76. London: SCM, 1958.

Vosloo, Robert. "Identity, Otherness and the Triune God: Theological Groundwork for a Christian Ethic of Hospitality." *Journal of Theology for Southern Africa* 119 (2004) 69–89.

Wesley, John. "Sermon LXV: The General Deliverance." In *Sermons on Several Occasions.* New York: Harper, 1827.

Widom, Cathy S., and Michael G. Maxfield. "An Update on the 'Cycle of Violence.'" *National Institute of Justice: Research in Brief,* February 2001. https://www.ncjrs.gov/ pdffiles1/nij/184894.pdf.

Wiesel, Elie. *Night.* New York: Hill & Wang, 1960.

Williams, Delores S. *Sisters in the Wilderness: The Challenge of Womanist God-Talk.* Maryknoll, NY: Orbis, 1993.

Wink, Walter. *Engaging the Powers: Discernment and Resistance in a World of Domination.* Minneapolis: Fortress, 1984.

Wirzba, Norman. "Reconciliation through Eating." In Fred Bahnson and Norman Wirzba, *Making Peace with the Land: God's Call to Reconcile with Creation,* 113–34. Downers Grove, IL: InterVarsity, 2012.

Woodley, Randy S. *Shalom and the Community of Creation: An Indigenous Vision.* Grand Rapids: Eerdmans, 2012.

World Health Organization. "Water-Related Diseases." http://www.who.int/water_ sanitation_health/diseases/malnutrition/en/.

Yordy, Laura Ruth. *Green Witness: Ecology, Ethics, and the Kingdom of God.* Eugene, OR: Cascade, 2008.

Zobel, H.-J. "הָדַר." In vol. 13 of *Theological Dictionary of the Old Testament,* edited by G. Johannes Botterweck and Helmer Ringgren, translated by David E. Green, 330–36. Grand Rapids: Eerdmans, 2004.

Index

Made in the USA
Middletown, DE
22 January 2018